Stakeholder Marketing

Stakeholder Marketing

Michelle Gledhill

AMSTERDAM • BOSTON • HEIDELBERG • LONDON • NEW YORK • OXFORD
PARIS • SAN DIEGO • SAN FRANCISCO • SINGAPORE • SYDNEY • TOKYO
Butterworth-Heinemann is an imprint of Elsevier

Butterworth-Heinemann is an imprint of Elsevier
The Boulevard, Langford Lane, Kidlington, Oxford, OX5 1GB, UK
30 Corporate Drive, Suite 400, Burlington, MA 01803, USA

First edition 2008

British Library Cataloguing in Publication Data
A catalogue record for this book is available from the British Library

Library of Congress Cataloguing in Publication Data
A catalogue record for this book is available from the Library of Congress

ISBN: 978-0-08-096626-7

For information on all Butterworth-Heinemann publications
visit our website at http://www.elsevierdirect.com

Printed and bound in Great Britain
10 11 12   10 9 8 7 6 5 4 3 2 1

Working together to grow
libraries in developing countries

www.elsevier.com | www.bookaid.org | www.sabre.org

ELSEVIER   BOOK AID International   Sabre Foundation

Contents

The Importance of Stakeholders

Learning outcomes

Assess the relative importance of organizational stakeholders on the marketing function and the impact they have on the organization's marketing activities.

Syllabus Content

1.1 Assess the different categories of relationships that exist between organizations.

1.2 Assess the relative importance of the different stakeholder groups and consider the nature of stakeholder relationships and their influence and impact on the organization.

1.3 Explain the nature of the interactions between the organization and its different stakeholders groups.

1.4 Explain the significance of the range of pressure groups as key stakeholders interested in the organization and their potential impacts upon market-oriented organizations.

1.5 Specify the role of marketing in managing these pressure groups effectively.

1.6 Evaluate the different options to developing a relationship management (RM) approach within a market-oriented organization.

RELATIONSHIPS BETWEEN ORGANIZATIONS

DEFINITION

Stakeholders are defined as:

Those persons and organizations that have an interest in the strategy of the organization. Stakeholders normally include shareholders, customers, staff and the local community. (CIMA)

As such we can consider stakeholders to be people and organizations who have a say in the following:

- What you are to do

- What resources you have

- What you should achieve.

They are affected by, and feel they have a right to benefit or be pleased by, what you do.

It is important to remember that if an organization tries to implement strategies which are in conflict with the interests of powerful stakeholders those strategies are highly likely to fail. This does mean, however, that if powerful stakeholders agree with what we are trying to do it will greatly improve our chances of success.

With that in mind, it is important for an organization to identify its stakeholders and their power to affect the decisions and outcomes. Within this process it is worth noting that stakeholder values may not be immediately apparent, and it is important to distinguish between desired, stated and lived values.

Much the same as in real life, when mapping stakeholders you should always consider that individuals might be members of more than one stakeholder group. For instance, an employee, who is a trade union member, may also be active in the local community. This would place that person in three different groups – which you might consider to have completely different values. It would be silly to think that the groups did not communicate with each other and form alliances or that the same person could be treated in different ways depending on which group you choose to include them in.

One-to-one relationships

This section looks at key 'boundary of the firm' decisions. These are the decisions a firm makes over whether to make components (or perform activities) itself, or whether to subcontract or outsource such production (or process) to a supplier.

The advantages of outsourcing are as follows:

- The opportunity of reducing cost by subcontracting to a specialist with economies of scope or scale.

- Receiving a better service/product as a result of the supplier's 'expert' status.

- Reduced management effort in planning, organizing and supervising the activity.

The disadvantages of outsourcing are as follows:

- Increased transaction costs, as a customer/supplier relationship is created.

- Risk that the supply might not meet the expectations in terms of cost, quality or delivery.

- Increased adversarial activity between the customer and supplier.

A competence is an activity or process through which an organization deploys or utilizes its resources. It is something the organization does, rather than something it has. Strategic competences can be classified as follows:

- Threshold competence is the level of competence necessary for an organization to compete and survive in a given industry and market. For example, an online bookseller must have a logistics system that allows books to be delivered as promised to the customers who have bought them.

- A core competence is something the organization does that underpins a source of competitive advantage. For example, if an online bookseller is able to deliver books a day or two earlier than its rivals, this represents a core competence.

Cox (1996) has developed a different way of looking at competences in terms of strategic supply chain management. He suggests that competences come in three types, as follows:

1. **Core competences** – These are areas where the organization should never consider outsourcing, as they are those competences that give a competitive advantage. In this case, the decision should always be to make or do.

2. **Complementary competences** – In this case, the firm should outsource but only to trusted key suppliers who have the skills to supply as required. The firm would also enter into a strategic relationship with the supplier.

3. **Residual competencies** – In these areas, the organization should outsource by means of an 'arm's length' relationship – a simple 'buy' decision.

Thus, when making strategic 'make/do or buy' decisions, the organization should determine what type of competence is being considered.

There are six available strategies for sourcing supplies, explained as follows:

1. **Adversarial procurement** – Is the typical competitive resource acquisition process, where the buyer puts pressure on the supplier to meet quality expectations at the lowest possible cost.

2. **Preferred supplier relationship** – Is where a small number of suppliers are given special status, and competition to supply is limited to these.

3. **Single sourcing** – Is where there is a 'sole supplier' relationship, with one key supplier and a blurring of the 'boundary of the firm'.

4. **Network sourcing** – Is where the organization creates a 'virtual company' at different stages of the supply chain by creating strategic partnerships at each stage.

5. **Acquisition** – Is where the organization vertically integrates with a supplier or suppliers.

6. **In-house process** – Is where the organization decides to retain responsibility for performing the process, rather than involving a supplier.

Quinn and Hilmer (1995) state four advantages of what they term 'strategic outsourcing':

1. Managers can concentrate their efforts on what the enterprise does best and therefore get the best returns on internal resources.

2. Well-developed core competences provide barriers to entry that can be used to protect competitive advantage.

3. Firms can fully leverage the investments, innovations and capabilities of their suppliers that would be prohibitively expensive or even impossible to duplicate in-house.

4. Such collaborative strategy decreases risk, shortens life cycles, and creates better responsiveness to changing customer needs.

In order to gain these benefits, Quinn and Hilmer suggest that organizations need to resolve three key issues:

1. What exactly are their core competences?

2. Having identified the core competences, should everything else be outsourced?

3. How can managers identify and manage the risks of those activities that are desirable to outsource?

Quinn and Hilmer put forward three tests to indicate whether any non-core activity should be outsourced:

1. What is the potential for gaining competitive advantage from this activity, taking into account transaction costs? The lower the potential, the more sensible it is to outsource.

2. What is the potential vulnerability to market failure that could arise if the activity were outsourced? Once again, the lower the risk, the more sensible it is to outsource.

3. What can be done to reduce these risks by structuring arrangements with suppliers in such a way as to protect ourselves? In this case, the more we can protect ourselves, the more sensible it is to outsource.

AstraZeneca outsourcing clinical data management

Clinical data management (CDM) is a critical part of the research and development process to get new drugs to the market. It ensures that data captured from clinical trials is used efficiently to determine the effectiveness of new medicines, which are then registered with the regulatory authorities. Streamlining this process gets products to be marketed more quickly.

Astra Zeneca runs around 150 studies a year, involving 50,000 patients in 50 countries. These generate around 1.5 million data sets annually. In 2007, it decided to outsource CDM. The sourcing process identified Cognizant as the right partner, and a contract was signed in 2007 with the service fully operational by mid-2008.

The benefits of the deal include a significant cost reduction over five years in AstraZeneca's cost base, a high quality delivery process measured by service-levels agreements and key performance indicators, a commitment from each company to invest in new technologies and processes and the effective cost control and visibility by means of the service order process.

Source: Supply Management 24.09.09

Relationship channels

DEFINITION

According to Handfield and Nichols (2002):
The supply chain encompasses all those organizations and activities associated with the flow and transformation of goods from the raw materials stage, through to the end user, as well as the associated information flow.

The same authors also define supply chain management (SCM) as:
The integration and management of supply chain organizations and activities through co-operative organizational relationships.

According to Jespersen and Skjott-Larsen (2005), 'The competitiveness of international companies is highly dependent on their ability to deliver customized products quickly and timely all over the World. Therefore, focus has moved from competition between firms at the same level in the production process to competition between supply chains, from raw materials to end customers.'

Linkages within a supply chain are either upstream or downstream. These terms relate to the 'direction of flow' in the supply chain, so downstream refers to towards the customer and upstream towards the supplier.

From a purchasing perspective, the supply chain processes are as follows:

- Search

- Acquire

- Use

- Maintain

- Dispose

From the supplying perspective, the processes are as follows:

- Research

- Design

- Manufacture or provide

- Sell

- Service

Supply chains are often described diagrammatically, as shown in Figure 1.1 below.

Of course, real supply chains are a lot more complicated than shown here. Suppliers and customers in a supply chain are often referred to as being in tiers. In the above diagram, the supplier would be a tier 1 supplier, and the supplier's supplier a tier 2 supplier.

According to Cox and Lamming (1997), this view of a supply chain being a series of dyadic (one-to-one) relationships is based on a model of business dating from the nineteenth century. At that time, 'the manner in which firms dealt with one another reflected their competencies' – in other words, each organization (or, more often, individuals) used their own skills as part of a 'joint wish to provide' products to the end consumer and a 'commercially based respect for the technical capabilities available from both companies' Mass production principles destroyed this model and replaced it with a high

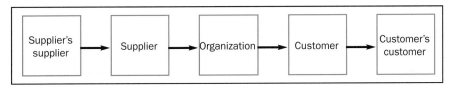

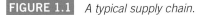

FIGURE 1.1 *A typical supply chain.*

volume model serving consumers that were 'easily led and presented manufacturers with a ready, tempting opportunity for exploitation'.

This meant, according to Cox and Lamming, that 'for the first three-quarters of the twentieth century, the mass producers could thus force their "vanilla" products upon their sales markets.' There was therefore no incentive for organizations to have any kind of sophisticated relationship with their 'compliant supply market', particularly where the purchaser had a wide spread of potential suppliers who could be controlled in one of two ways:

1. By being bought, leading to the development of vertically integrated 'mass production leviathans'.

2. By extracting their expertise under threat of the loss of business.

There is some academic argument as to whether it is reasonable to view the supply chain as a chain. Indeed, many definitions cannot help referring to the supply chain as something other than a chain. For example, 'a supply chain is a network of organizations that . . .'

Relationship networks

According to Harland (1996), there are four different applications of the term 'supply chain':

1. The internal supply chain, which integrates business functions involved in the flow of materials and information from 'inbound' to 'outbound'.

2. A dyadic (or two-party relationship) between a supplier and a customer.

3. A series of businesses, including a firm, its supplier, its supplier's supplier, its customer and its customer's customer, etc.

4. A network of interconnected businesses involved in the ultimate provision of product and service packages required by end customers.

According to Hakansson (1987) a network is based on linkages between actors, resources and activities, as follows:

- Actors may range from individuals to groups of companies, but they all aim to increase their control of the network. They perform activities and own and control resources (either singly or jointly).

- Resources may be human or physical and are often mutually dependent. They are owned by actors and are either used in the performance of activities or are the subject of those activities.

- Activities include those concerned with transformation and those with transaction. Activities use and act on resources and are performed by actors.

There are a number of reasons why we should regard supply chains as networks:

- We are more likely to take a supply-chain-wide view when formulating strategy, rather than just concentrating on tier 1 suppliers and customers.

- We should become more responsive and innovative, as the supply chain is better informed and can react in a consistent manner.

- Throughput times will be shortened, leading to a reduction in inventory levels throughout the chain and subsequent improvements in cashflows and margins.

- Inter-firm relations are more likely to be mutually beneficial, leading to more stable supply chains and improved service levels.

INSIGHT: Protect your supply

During a recession public sector buyers are presented with a paradox to squeeze value from public procurement whist demand for public services such as job centres, policing, health and social care is increasing. The focus, therefore, is not just on cutting cost, but delivering more for the customer.

Never before has strategic procurement been so essential in the public sector. Risk management is now more rigorous and involves assessing the potential consequences of a supplier going bust; ranking suppliers according to that risk analysing the financial availability of critical suppliers, and diversifying supply bases to ensure continuity. For example, in the Department for

Work and Pensions (DWP) most areas of the provision, including buildings, IT, telephony and the electronic payment systems for benefits are outsourced. They are also using more advanced tools for measuring financial liability, including formulas that assess the financial health of a company and predict the probability of bankruptcy. Traditionally, purchasers have used credit reference agencies such as Dunn and Bradstreet and Experian to assess the financial viability of companies. But the recession and banking crisis developed the validity of these scores came into question.

As suppliers hit hard times, how far should buyers go in extending support to them? And to what extent should the government's £175 billion spend on goods and services act as a force for good in the economy by helping keep suppliers afloat. Lee Tribe, the director of commercial strategy and development at DWP, asserts that they have an obligation to look after major suppliers in times of financial crisis but how far this support extends through the supply chain is undecided.

Public sector purchasing can make a difference to suppliers' liquidity by improving payment terms. Lord Mandelson has announced measures to help small firms weather the credit crunch. These included paying invoices within 10 days to ease cash flow.

Procurement can also support suppliers by opening contracts to a wider field. Portsmouth City Council works with Business Link and the Chamber of commerce to promote contract opportunities to local suppliers through 'meet the buyer ' events. It also advertises on the council's website and links sub-contractors with prime contractors delivering the council's Building Schools for the future programme online.

The Glover Review recommended helping small businesses secure better access to public contracts. By 2010 public sector contracts worth more than £20,000 will be advertised in a single free online portal, and measures to educe bureaucracy and make opportunities more transparent will be introduced.

Suppliers have become more demanding as a result of being under greater financial strain and uncertainty. Hammersmith and Fulham Borough Council is moving to a new social care model that involves giving money to some clients so they can buy and manage their own social care. Previously suppliers would have coped with the transition themselves but now they are asking the council for more support and time.

The drive for efficiency in public procurement will continue unabated in order to release cash in frontline services. In 2007 government set itself the target of delivering £30 billion of efficiency savings over a three-year period. This has been extended by an extra £5 billion in a bid to boost the economy. As a result of these targets, all levels of government are already under significant pressure to reduce costs and improve efficiency.

Source: Supply Management, April 2009

STAKEHOLDER GROUPS AND RELATIONSHIPS

Stakeholder maps/matrices
Freeman – stakeholder mapping

DEFINITION

Freeman (1984) defined a stakeholder as:
Any group or individual who can affect or is affected by the achievement of the organization's objectives.

Thus, a group qualifies as a stakeholder if it has a legitimate interest in aspects of the organization's activities and thus, according to Freeman, has either the power to affect the firm's performance and/or has a stake in the firm's performance. This definition implies two types of stakeholders – strategic and moral. The strategic stakeholders – the ones who can affect a firm – and their interests must be 'dealt with' so that the firm may still achieve its objectives. For the moral stakeholder – the one who is affected by the firm – stakeholder theorists seek some accommodation or alignment of interests. Freeman's focus is on how executives can use the theory, framework, philosophy and processes of the stakeholder approach to manage their organizations more effectively.

To implement stakeholder theory, the first of Freeman key concepts requires the organization to have a full appreciation of all the persons or groups who have interests in planning, process(es), delivery and/or outcomes of the product or service. This process of identifying and classifying stakeholders has led to the development of stakeholder mapping. According to Freeman, the purpose of the stakeholder map is to identify all the 'generic stakeholders', that is, those categories of groups who can affect the organization.

Conventionally, a stakeholder map is drawn with the organization at the centre, with the various stakeholder groups radiating around it like the spokes of a wheel (Figure 1.2). An example, applied to a supermarket, is shown in Figure 1.3 below.

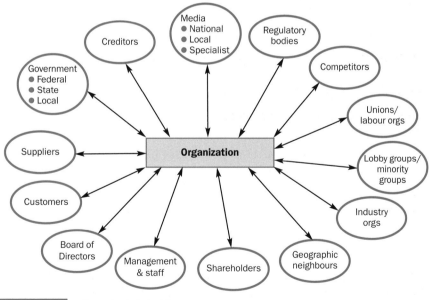

FIGURE 1.2   *Generic stakeholder map.*

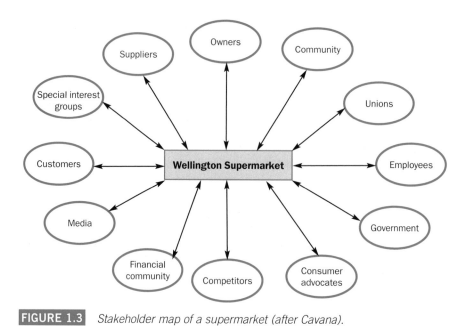

FIGURE 1.3 *Stakeholder map of a supermarket (after Cavana).*

MENDELOW'S POWER-INTEREST MATRIX

Power is the potential ability of an individual or group to exert an influence on others to persuade them into following a particular course of action. This means that those who have power have the potential to influence behaviour, to change the course of events, to overcome resistance and to persuade people to do things that they might not otherwise do.

Power comes from a number of sources, and only some of them have anything to do with the individual's position in the organization. Although there are many ways that sources of power may be described, the following categorization encompasses most definitions:

- **Positional power** – This arises because of an individual's position in an organizational hierarchy and is reflected in their formal authority and reputation.

- **Resource power** – This arises because an individual can control, obtain or create resources or other items of value. Those items of value need not necessarily be tangible; they can be affection or a sense of belonging to a particular group. This affords the holder the ability to reward, coerce or punish those over whom the power is exercised.

- **System power** – This arises because an individual is central to a group, has political access, has high visibility and relevance to a particular situation. This is sometimes known as network power because the individual who wields the power is 'connected' to the right people.

- **Expert power** – This arises because an individual has information, knowledge, expertise and professional credibility and fits with the organization's requirements.

- **Personal power** – This form of power arises because an individual has charisma, energy, attractiveness, determination, communication skills, personal reputation or the ability to confront. Quite often this will be a person who is self-effacing and is able to let others take the credit for a success. This is sometimes known as charismatic power.

It is worth remembering that

- Power is exercised by individuals, not groups, and is invariably personalized in some way. The power will only be effective if an individual exercises it over another individual or group.

- Power is based on a system of ideas and a body of common knowledge. The leaders or the other person's power is dependent upon their success in developing and convincingly communicating a clear and compelling message that embodies the core system of ideas and the new body of common knowledge. The message must be powerful and simple enough to overcome competing messages.

- Although power is exercised by individuals it is exercised through organizations, and its exercise is legitimized and constrained by the organization's common knowledge. Some type of organization, institution or group is necessary for the enduring exercise of power.

- Power actions occur in a context that includes various stakeholders and audiences. Any important stakeholder group or significant body of opinion must be involved in some way. However, a leader's power can be extended to larger groups or organizations by delegation.

- Power vacuums occur when power is not exercised or is abused, resulting in the increased incidence, and cost, of conflict and other

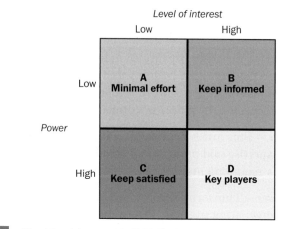

FIGURE 1.4 *The Mendelow matrix (1991) Aubrey Mendelow.*

problems such as poor quality, lowered productivity and decreased adaptability to change.

Once the power and expectations (and therefore their likely interest) have been established, we can use a power interest matrix to assist the analysis. Mendelow (1991) has proposed such a matrix (Figure 1.4).

If the stakeholders are plotted regularly, this matrix can be used to determine the potential influence of stakeholder groups. As strategies are proposed or modified by the organization, the matrix can be used to highlight possible threats (or assistance) from particular stakeholders groups.

We will look in Unit 2 at the detail of how the matrix can be used.

The block matrix

To build a capacity to influence an individual or organization, it is helpful to analyse the extent to which there is trust and agreement between the two of you:

- Trust can be defined as 'our capacity to believe that a person will follow through on the commitments they make'.

- Agreement can be defined as 'our belief that a person shares with us a common commitment to important outcomes'.

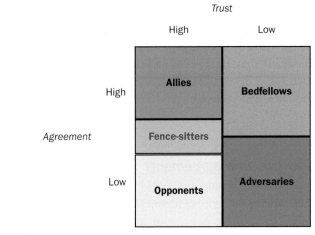

FIGURE 1.5 *Block matrix.*

Taken together, there are (according to Block – see Figure 1.5) five political labels that can assist us in evaluating how and what we need to do to influence the behaviour of those important to our work. Each label describes a different blend of trust and agreement.

Allies (high trust/high agreement)

Allies are people we agree with regarding important issues and trust to follow through on their commitments. They are our strongest supporters and can be used to influence other parties.

Bedfellows (low trust/high agreement)

Bedfellows are people who agree with us but whom we do not trust to follow through on their agreements. They may be afraid to rock the boat or have different priorities from us. We should aim to turn them into allies.

Fence-sitters (fluctuating trust and agreement)

Fence-sitters are people whose positions, goals and values are unclear and who are not convincing when they express support. Their position and actions can change and, as a result, we do not trust them when they agree that our position is important.

Opponents (high trust/low agreement)

Opponents are people we trust but disagree with. We know they will be honest with us and may be willing to negotiate, but we may never be able to persuade them that our views are right as this would mean that their views are wrong. They will be up front and open in expressing their views, which makes them easier to deal with than adversaries or fence-sitters.

Adversaries (low trust/low agreement)

Adversaries are people we do not trust and do not agree with on important issues. They withhold information, lie and go behind our backs. This might lead us to want to behave in kind. Others who observe this type of behaviour learn that we are capable of being unworthy of trust and, as a result, we can lose the trust of our colleagues and important stakeholders.

THE ORGANIZATION AND ITS STAKEHOLDERS

Interactions between the organization and its stakeholders

Based on the Block matrix, explained in the previous section, a number of different approaches to stakeholder interaction may be appropriate.

Allies (high trust/high agreement)

The most appropriate way to treat allies is to

- Affirm agreement on the project or relationship by keeping in close contact and stressing shared values.

- Reaffirm the quality of the relationship by expressing trust and reminding the ally of the strength of the relationship.

- Acknowledge any doubts and vulnerabilities that the ally might express about the relationship.

- Ask the ally for advice, particularly on aspects of the relationship that might reduce trust or lead to disagreement.

Bedfellows (low trust/high agreement)

The most appropriate way to treat bedfellows is to

- Reaffirm agreement on the project or relationship by keeping in close contact and stressing shared values.
- Acknowledge the caution that exists and express reservations about the failings or shortcomings of past discussions.
- Be clear about what is wanted from both parties in working together.
- Try to reach an agreement about the process of working together.
- Deliver on promises to increase trust.

Fence-sitters (fluctuating trust and agreement)

The most appropriate way to treat fence-sitters is to

- State your position in the relationship or project clearly to ensure agreement is possible.
- Ask them where they stand, seeking their agreement to small issues in order to move towards agreement on the 'big issue'.
- Apply gentle pressure on them to change their views and move towards agreement.
- Express mild frustration about their neutrality but avoid antagonizing them.
- Encourage them to be transparent about what it would take to have them reach an agreement.
- Deliver on promises to increase trust.

Opponents (high trust/low agreement)

The most appropriate way to treat opponents is to

- Reaffirm the quality of the relationship and remind them that it is based on mutual trust (despite your difference of opinion).
- State your position, so they clearly understand your vision, purpose and goals.

- State (in neutral way) what you think their position is and seek clarification.

- Understand their position and respect their views.

- Engage in a problem-solving process, with a view to negotiating the shared steps to a mutually acceptable end point.

Adversaries (low trust/low agreement)

The most appropriate way to treat adversaries is to

- State your position, so they clearly understand your vision, purpose and goals.

- State (in a neutral way) what you think their position is and seek clarification.

- Understand their position and respect their views.

- State your contribution to the problem.

- End meetings with plans and action lists, but make no demands on them.

- Enlist a party trusted by your adversary to act as mediator and to vouch for your trustworthiness.

- Deliver on promises to increase trust.

- Do not spend too much time obsessing about the relationship, as the most likely result is that they become an opponent or bedfellow.

CASE STUDY: Backing the Future

Sustainability will be a key issue over the next decade, shaping government policy, business strategy and how we live our lives.

As the world's population grows by billions and the Western way of consumption is adopted by hundreds of millions of people in the developing world, we are running out of the basics – trees, clean water, farmland and so on. Meanwhile, we are driving changes to our climate at a rate not seen for many thousands of years.

So, what has all this got to do with marketing? First, businesses will have to adapt to this challenge, telling stories about the sustainable products and services they will be developing. Moreover, we believe that communication, even more than technology, is the key to building a sustainable future.

To illustrate why, we are going to share five key lessons from M&S' sustainability journey. It is important to stress the word 'journey', as no business in the world can claim to have come remotely close to sustainability.

The first lesson is not unique to M&S. Many global businesses, including Nike, Unilever and Google, have recognised that the days of corporate social responsibility (CSR) are over.

CSR was all about managing a few sensitive areas that had the potential to generate positive or negative headlines. To be a credible player today, however, you have to understand all the social and environmental issues that are relevant to your business.

To tackle these, you need a clear business case, commitment from the top and alignment throughout the ranks. This covers not only your own operations, but also your supply chain and the way your customers use your products.

In 2006, M&S recognised that it needed to start working systemically to make its business more sustainable by addressing the social and environmental issues on which it had an impact. These span our supply chains (thousands of factories and farms), our own operations (hundreds of stores and lorries) and the use of the millions of products we sell each year. M&S then made 100 commitments related to these issues.

Lesson number two: we did not call this approach 'the M&S' sustainability plan'. We gave it instead the much more memorable name 'Plan A' – because there is no Plan B when it comes to saving the planet. We hit on the name only two weeks before launch, when our then head of internal communication, Robert Nuttall, raised the concern that we had a great idea but no inspiration. Our communications teams developed the Plan A brand and, in one fell swoop, our task was made much easier.

Internally, Plan A has been a powerful change brand, helping 75,000 M&S employees and 2000 suppliers to see the links between activities as disparate as taking trans fats out of food, reducing energy use and promoting Fairtrade.

Externally it has allowed us to demonstrate to stakeholders and the 10 per cent of our customers who are 'green crusaders' that M&S is committed to playing a leading role on sustainability.

However, lesson number three is that Plan A is not a consumer-facing brand. For 18 months we thought it was, but we struggled to bring our stories to life for our mainstream customers. Plan A was an improvement on 'M&S' sustainability plan', but it was not enough to connect with 90 per cent of our customers.

Earlier this year, our marketing team developed a customer strapline for our Plan A activities – 'Doing the right thing'. Our customers could connect with this simple sentiment that summed up our reasons for selling only Fairtrade coffee and tea, or using only free-range eggs.

However, even more important learning was emerging. Lesson four is that consumers buy more deeply into sustainability when they are engaged in change, and not just told about it. We know that consumers want business to do the 'heavy lifting' on sustainability, but you get more traction when consumers are given the opportunity to make some easy contributions themselves.

Questions

1. Conduct a Block Matrix for M&S.

2. Assess M&S's approach to stakeholder management and interaction using the political labels identified in the Block matrix.

ACTIVITY

Construct a Block matrix for your organization.

PRESSURE GROUPS

Pressure groups and their impact

A pressure group (sometimes known as an advocacy group, a lobby group, an interest group or a special interest group) is an organized collection of people who seek to influence political decisions and policy, without seeking election to public office. Pressure groups are a component of any pluralist democracy and are of three types

1. Sectional groups represent the interests of their members. They include the following:

   - Business groups, such as the Confederation of British Industry

   - Professional bodies, such as the British Medical Association

   - Trades unions.

   Aside from representing the interest of their members, these groups may have influence on broader issues and may be led by political ideology, such as socialism for the Transport and General Workers' Union in the United Kingdom.

2. Causal groups (also known as promotional or attitude groups) seek to influence policy in a particular area, such as the environment (Greenpeace), gun laws (National Rifle Association) or the protection of birds (Royal Society for the Protection of Birds, the largest advocacy group in Europe). These tend to be aligned towards a political ideology or seek influence in other policy areas.

3. 'Fire brigade' groups lobby on a specific issue such as the War in Iraq or the Poll Tax. They usually disband as soon as the issue has been resolved.

A group may have more influence, if it has a large membership, adequate funding, reflects public opinion or is supported by the media. Trades unions also have the sanction of being able to strike, and other groups can organize demonstrations.

The main function of interest groups is to provide information. They provide information to politicians, executive agencies and to constituents. There are three types of information acquired by interest groups. They are as follows:

1. The status and prospect of bills under active consideration.

2. The electoral implications of legislators' support or opposition to potential legislation.

3. The political, economic, social and environmental consequences of policies.

Aside from advocacy, interest groups are often engaged in service delivery of some kind, often to their members. They also engage in the marketing of their 'cause'.

Sectional pressure groups

The Marketing Society

The Marketing Society is 'the most influential network of senior marketers dedicated to championing marketing in the UK'.

The Marketing Society's manifesto outlines how marketers must adopt new roles in their organizations. They must become the customer champions, business innovators and growth drivers. They must also become more accountable, collaborative and commercial.

The Law Society

The Law Society of England and Wales is the professional association that represents the solicitors' profession in England and Wales. It provides services and support to practising and training solicitors and also serves as a sounding board for law reform. Often, members of the Society are consulted when important issues are being debated in Parliament or by the executive.

The TUC

The Trades Union Congress (TUC) is the voice of Britain at work. With 66 affiliated unions representing nearly 7 million working people from all walks of life, it campaigns for a fair deal at work and for social justice at home and abroad. The TUC negotiates in Europe and in the UK builds links with political parties, business, local communities and wider society.

The TUC

- Brings Britain's unions together to draw up common policies

- Lobbies the government to implement policies that will benefit people at work

- Campaigns on economic and social issues

- Represents working people on public bodies

- Represents British workers in international bodies, in the European Union and at the UN employment body – the International Labour Organization

- Carries out research on employment-related issues

- Runs an extensive training and education programme for union representatives

- Helps unions develop new services for their members

- Helps unions avoid clashes with each other

- Builds links with other trade union bodies worldwide.

Chambers of Commerce

The British Chambers of Commerce (BCC) is the national body for a powerful and influential Network of Accredited Chambers of Commerce across the UK. The BCC is a non-political, non-profit-making organization, owned and directed by its members, democratically accountable to individual businesses of all sizes and sectors throughout the UK. Every Chamber sits at the very heart of its local business community, reaching the entire business community and providing services, information and guidance to its members. No other UK business organization represents its network and members at such senior levels of UK decision making, working with government to shape policy affecting UK businesses.

The BCC claims to be

- The voice of UK business

- The partner of first choice for information and guidance

- The natural choice for business support.

Pressure Groups in Action

The National Farmers' Union (NFU) at the 2009 IGD conference called on retailers to develop a consistent, industry-wide carbon-labelling system for product packaging. Tesco, which recently unveiled plans to display the 'carbon footprint' on the packaging of 500 products supported the calls for a consistent approach.

Source: Marketing 21.10.09

Causal pressure groups

Welfare

Welfare pressure groups seek to further the interests of a section of society or a 'voiceless' group such as animals. Among such main groups in the UK are the following:

- Fathers 4 Justice
- Society for the Protection of Unborn Children
- National Society for the Prevention of Cruelty to Children (NSPCC)
- British Union for the Abolition of Vivisection
- League Against Cruel Sports
- Royal Society for the Prevention of Cruelty to Animals
- Scottish Society for the Prevention of Cruelty to Animals
- Countryside Alliance.

INSIGHT

Garston Park is a small urban park in South Liverpool. It is the site for the local leisure centre and car park but also contains football pitches, a small children's playground, exercise equipment along a path, a bowling green and associated hut, benches and trees. The edges of the park tend to be more 'natural' with longer grass and some flowers. There is no fence around the park which is bounded by four residential streets.

Garston Park (also known as Long Lane Rec) is the property of Liverpool City Council which carries out general maintenance and improvements.

In 2009, a group called Friends of Garston Park was formed to give more of a sense of local ownership and involvement around the park. The Friends have a number of aims including following:

* to act as consultees when Liverpool City Council makes proposals about the park
* to raise money and carry out improvements supported by local people
* to help promote and protect the park

To date two planting sessions have been organised, planting crocus bulbs in two 'end' locations.

Plans for the future include the following:

* funding planters for floral displays at the main entrance (where the path starts)

* a general meeting to ensure major community consultation about the park and its future
* lobbying the Council for improvements to the children's play area
* wildflower and quiet areas to be extended in parts of the park

The Friends are now members of the Liverpool Park Friends Forum. The Friends meet monthly inviting local residents and relevant experts to meetings.

INSIGHT

Introducing the 2010–2016 strategy, NSPCC Chief Executive Andrew Flanagan, said,

'The NSPCC and all who work and support the Society are inspired by a belief that we can make a difference for all children – by standing up for their rights, by listening to them, by helping them when they need us and by making them safe.'

The strategy is built on 4 key principles:

Focus – Providing well-defined and distinct activities where the impact for children can be maximized, e.g Children's Voice Appeal

Prioritize – Concentrating on specific types of abuse and on children who are at most risk to ensure intervention creates the greatest impact e.g Kicking, Bullying Into Touch Challenge.

Learning – Everything the NSPCC will do will create learning. The NSPCC must capture that learning and use it to create a cycle of improvement, e.g NSPCC Inform

Leverage – On its own the NSPCC cannot end cruelty to children. The Society needs to work with and through others to multiply its impact many times over, e.g. Fashion designer Jeff Banks has called on the nation to join the NSPCC Great British Clothes Clearout and donate their unwanted clothes to raise £2m for the NSPCC by 2012.

Source: www.nspcc.org.uk

Fair trade and environmental

Environmental groups seek to protect or enhance some aspect of the natural world. These include the following:

- Campaign for the Protection of Rural England
- Campaign for the Protection of Rural Wales

- Greenpeace

- Friends of the Earth

- Transport 2000 (an anti-car group)

- Countryside Alliance

- The Campaign for Real Ale (CAMRA).

Impacts
Change in strategy

It is not just direct influence that organizations have to contend with. Pressure groups also lobby governments, and this may have a significant indirect impact on strategy, through new or changed legislation and government policy. In the United States, pressure groups can exert significant influence in this way.

Development of new products and services

Pressure groups have often changed not just the way organizations work but also the very products they produce. Think about the development of recycled and recyclable products on sale or the development of 'hybrid' cars that run on electricity as well as other fuel.

It is not just products but also services that are affected. If you take a flight with many air carriers, you are given the option, when buying your ticket, to sponsor some sort of 'carbon offset' activity such as conservation work or tree planting. While some consumers may be sceptical about the legitimacy of such schemes, environmentally based products and services are one of the fastest growing sectors. The Forestry Stewardship Council (FSC) developed a certification scheme promoting products sourced from sustainability-managed forests. The FSC has had a significant impact, spawning a number of rival schemes and influencing procurement practices for governments as well as small businesses.

Many consumers are too young to remember a world without 'green' detergents. This was one of the first industries to respond to pressure to reduce the pollution and environmental damage caused by excessive detergent use. Washing machine manufacturers now design machines to use less water and less electricity, as well as persuade us to wash our clothes at lower temperatures. In this latter effort, they have been supported by detergent manufacturers, who have developed new 'low temperature' products.

INSIGHT

In the never-ending effort to improve the performance of appliances, two Japanese companies have come up with the idea of applying ultrasound to washing machines, though they came up with very different applications of the technology.

Sanyo recently put on sale a washing machine that does not require detergent to clean lightly soiled clothes. The machine is fitted with electrodes on the side of the tub that electrolyse the water, and an ultrasonic wave generator at the base of the machine. The ultrasonic waves, which are essentially millions of tiny air bubbles, help loosen grime and grit on clothes in a purely mechanical action.

Electrolysing the water produces active oxygen, or forms of oxygen such as hydrogen peroxide and ozone, and hypochlorous acid, a mild bleaching agent. Hypochlorous acid kills bacteria, while active oxygen dissolves such dirt as the residue of body sweat. Sanyo claims this is enough for cleaning shirts, underwear, and towels soiled primarily by perspiration. Detergent can be used in the machine to clean clothes heavily stained with dirt or grease.

Sanyo claims users can halve the cost of doing normal laundry. Reducing the amount of detergent sent into waste water streams is also environmentally friendly. Currently, the 8kg load capacity washer is only available in Japan.

Rather than applying ultrasound waves on the entire wash, Sharp chose to use the technology in a spot washer intended to remove rings of dirt from collars and other stains. The Sharp washer features a small ultrasound generator that mounts in an arm positioned over a tray above the washer tub. Users position the stained part of the fabric between the washing head on the arm and a small trough on the tray, something like positioning fabric under a sewing machine needle.

With the trough filled with water, the fabric is saturated. The washer head oscillates up and down 34,000 times per second. On the downstroke, water molecules are pushed away; on the upstroke, cavitation results in cavities in the water. As these cavities combine and explode within the fabric fibre, stain-causing particles are blown away. After treating the stains, the garment is washed normally. The ultrasound arm and tray can be folded away.

Like Sanyo, the company currently has no plans to offer the machine outside Japan.

Process change

The biggest impact of pressure groups on business processes has come from the trade unions. Virtually every major piece of UK employment legislation has been directly influenced (and sometimes sponsored) either by individual unions or the TUC.

The activities of unions in respect of working processes impact on the following areas:

- **Issues of respect** – Workers are often mistreated by the boss through verbal or physical abuse: from constantly degrading remarks to sexual harassment and assault to a complete lack of empowerment, never listening to workers' suggestions.

- **Wage and benefits** – The vast majority of workers are not paid according to the full value of what they produce. Further, as inflation eats into the value of their wage, workers constantly have to fight for increases in pay and benefits. Workers who do not get these annual rises are in fact being paid less money (even though their wage remains the same) since the value of money is continually decreasing.

- **Hours worked** – Unions can force the boss to hire more workers, instead of constantly increasing the burdens on existing employees. The union can also ensure that in emergency cases where someone must work overtime, they are fairly compensated for (contrary to popular understanding, overtime compensation is compulsory for unskilled workers in only a handful of countries).

- **Working conditions** – Many workers do not work in a healthy or safe workplace environment. There is sometimes little prevention of potential dangers; protective gear is often old and ragged, and there can be various factors (high stress) leading to psychological problems. Occupational health and safety is the most unifying issue a union can pursue: even the most conservative workers can get totally irate if they believe that their health and safety are being threatened. Legally binding standards can often result from such struggles, which means that when they are enforced, a union delivers real benefits for their members, while winning to its ranks people who would otherwise never join a union.

- **Job security** – In many countries, a boss can fire workers at will, for no reason at all. A few countries, however, have laws against firing workers without due cause, and some countries do not allow firing to take place based on discrimination or union organizing, but that does not stop the boss from firing that same worker for any other reason. With a union, any disciplinary action taken against a worker may be subject to a procedure negotiated with the union, which guarantees a level of natural justice through union representation.

INSIGHT

The UK's 568,000 bar, pub and club workers are being subjected to music so loud that they could lose or permanently damage their hearing, according to a report published by deaf people's advocacy charity RNID and the TUC. 'Noise overload' shows that music played in UK nightclubs is so loud that in some cases it is like working next to an airplane taking off. The report argues that not enough is being done to protect the hearing of bar, club and pub workers from music played well above legal safe levels. It adds that local authorities are failing to enforce the noise-at-work regulations under which employers have a legal duty to protect their employees' hearing. Frances O'Grady, TUC deputy general secretary, said: 'Ear-splitting noise levels are deafening and damaging the hearing of the UK's bars, clubs and pubs workers. Employers can take simple steps to reduce the damage being done to staff without turning clubs into libraries. But it is up to local authorities to monitor and enforce the rules put in place to protect employees from noise overload.' RNID's Mark Hoda said: 'Because noise damage is cumulative and the effects not immediate, employers often fail to enforce hearing protection for their staff. And yet, a simple measure of wearing quality earplugs would protect these workers from long-term irreparable hearing damage. With Christmas just

around the corner, giving all bar staff quality earplugs would be the best present a bar or club owner could offer.'

Source: TUC

Negative publicity

One of the clearest examples of negative publicity affecting business has been in connection with genetically engineered (GE) foods. While most activists agree that they are up against a formidable opponent in corporate giants like Monsanto, Dupont, Cargill, Dow and Novartis, they point out that many of the companies are already moving away from biotech agriculture. Monsanto is under pressure from investors to sell off its life sciences division in response to the public controversy over GE food. Grain manufacturers are beginning to separate transgenic seeds as farmers reject the crops. McDonalds recently announced it would stop using genetically engineered potatoes to make french fries, and Frito Lays says it will ban the use of transgenic corn in its chips. And Gerber and Heinz have pledged to remove GE ingredients from baby food.

INSIGHT

About a dozen demonstrators dressed in mock biohazard suits dump food products from Safeway supermarket shelves into a plastic bin in front of the Marriott Hotel in this quiet suburban town East of San Francisco. Inside Safeway shareholders are set to vote on a resolution asking the nation's third largest supermarket chain to remove genetically engineered (GE) ingredients from its products. TV cameras roll while an organizer explains that the crackers, cereal, soda, macaroni and cheese, and other products contain genetically

engineered ingredients. One demonstrator wearing monarch butterfly wings – symbolizing a local species endangered by GE corn – looks on. Another carries a toddler on her hip.

Although Safeway shareholders rejected the resolution, as expected – less than the 3 per cent required to reintroduce it next year supported the resolution – organizers say their fight has just begun.

Source: CorpWatch

Decrease in share price

The end result of the activity of pressure groups has to be one of two things; either organizations change the products that they make or the processes they perform, or they will suffer a downturn in stakeholder confidence and a consequent reduction in shareholder value.

INSIGHT

BAE Systems'share price fell by 1 per cent, or 7p, to 502.5p after two pressure groups won permission to bring a High Court challenge over the decision to end investigations into alleged bribery and corruption involving the company and Saudi Arabia.

Source: Reuters, 9 November 2007

MARKETING AND PRESSURE GROUPS

The role of marketing in managing pressure groups

Most organizations adopt a reactive approach to the management of pressure groups. The result of this is that the organization finds itself continually 'firefighting' the effects of pressure group activity and trying to limit the impact of bad publicity.

A better approach is to be proactive in the management of such groups and to undertake marketing activity that fits with a relationship marketing approach towards pressure group stakeholders. This activity can take two forms:

1. Planned and continual marketing communications aimed at developing relationships with pressure group stakeholders. This might reduce the likelihood of any adverse pressure group activity.

2. Contingency planning, in advance of any issue, to respond in a prompt and professional manner. This might reduce the impact of any adverse pressure group activity.

One marketing guru has outlined a strategy on how organizations can defeat public interest activists, who apparently fall into four distinct categories:

- Radicals should be isolated and discredited.

- Opportunists should be ignored or treated as radicals.

- Idealists should be cultivated and educated into becoming realists.

- Realists can be engaged in rational dialogue and hopefully co-opted into agreeing with the organization.

Planned marketing communications
Public relations

> **DEFINITION**
>
> *Public relations is a set of management, supervisory, and technical functions that foster an organization's ability to strategically listen to, appreciate, and respond to those persons whose mutually beneficial relationships with the organization are necessary if it is to achieve its missions and values.*
>
> (Robert L. Heath, Encyclopaedia of Public Relations)

The four main roles of public relations are as follows:

1. To provide information to external stakeholders
2. To forge links with the organization's 'community'
3. To encourage good publicity
4. To negate bad publicity.

It is fairly obvious from this that the public relations function is likely to be the primary point of contact for pressure groups. Specific PR activities that might be targeted at pressure groups would include the following:

- Press releases
- Podcasts and webcasts
- Publishing of information material
- Internet placement
- Entertainment product placement (television, events, celebrity)
- Product launches
- Press conferences
- Producing events
- Establishing community relationships.

The detailed role of PR is explored in the following sections, which relate to specific communications tools.

Advertising

Advertising messages can mean very different things to different people. What a consumer finds interesting and informative, a pressure group might see as ammunition against the organization. It is therefore important that any advertising copy is 'vetted' for potentially dangerous copy before approval.

Brochures

While advertising messages, and particularly those using TV and radio, are transient, brochures tend to have a much longer 'shelf life'. A similar vetting approach is therefore recommended when producing any 'glossy' medium. This is just as true about a company's annual financial report as it is about a product catalogue. One of the ironies of corporate communications is that some sectors of the audience will invest more time and effort in analysing the content of a document than the organization did in producing it.

Encouraging interaction and dialogue

In the UK, the Institute of Public Relations has published a book on *Managing Activism* (Deegan, 2001), which outlines how companies can deal with activists and pressure groups. The way forward, argues the author, is 'proactive dialogue, negotiation and conflict resolution' or in PR jargon 'two-way symmetrical communications'. The book contains a number of suggestions for developing such dialogue, including the following:

- Hosting regular events for pressure group members, where the organization's views and activities can be communicated.

- Maintaining a network of personal relationships with activists to ensure that dialogue is possible even when views differ or are opposed.

- Co-opting individual activists to work on the organization's behalf.

Product messages

Design, durability and technical features

Products are the 'public face' of an organization. Many customers and consumers recognize an organization's products but are unaware of the producer's identity. When designing products, organizations should be aware of the potential for adverse PR impact of those products in the following areas:

- **Safety** – Particularly relating to safety for 'vulnerable groups' such as children and animals. Examples include ensuring that products do not have small parts that might be swallowed by children (toys) and ensuring that products are not toxic (foods).

- **Quality** – Products must not only be fit for purpose at the time of their purchase but must also maintain that fitness for a reasonable period. Examples include ensuring that electrical components continue to work for the expected lifetime of the product and that they do not degrade and become dangerous.

- **Packaging** – Should not be 'excessive' (think about Easter eggs, or many convenience food products), as this is likely to prompt adverse reaction from conservation bodies. It should also be safe, particularly if packaging cannot be recycled and will end up in landfill. Packaging should also secure any potentially dangerous products (think medicines and cleaning products).

- **Usability** – The functionality of product packaging may seem reasonable for those who test it but may prove impossible for sectors of the market. The elderly, for example, often complain about not being able to open food packaging (such as cans, jars and 'tear here' cellophane).

Production processes and distribution

With the increasing attention paid to environmental issues, organizations now have to consider the environmental impact of production and distribution processes. The excessive use of fossil fuels in producing and transporting products is likely to attract the attention of pressure groups. This aspect also provides an opportunity to organizations, as many consumers are starting to favour 'local' or 'low impact' products. This is particularly the case in foods, where customers are returning to seasonal foods, rather than accepting 'out of season' alternatives that have been transported from the opposite hemisphere of the globe.

There is also the issue of exploitation in the production process.

INSIGHT

Nike, long the subject of sweatshop allegations, yesterday produced the most comprehensive picture yet of the 700 factories that produce its footwear and clothing, detailing admissions of abuses, including forced overtime and restricted access to water.

The company has published a 108-page report, available on its website, the first since it paid $1.5m to settle allegations that it had made false claims about how well its workers were treated.

For years activists have been pressing Nike and other companies to reveal where their factories are in order to allow independent monitoring.

Nike lists 124 plants in China contracted to make its products, 73 in Thailand, 35 in South Korea, 34 in Vietnam and others in Asia. It also produces goods in South America, Australia, Canada, Italy, Mexico, Turkey and the United States. It employs 650,000 contract workers worldwide.

The report admits to widespread problems, particularly in Nike's Asian factories. The company said it audited hundreds of factories in 2003 and 2004 and found cases of 'abusive treatment', physical and verbal, in more than a quarter of its south Asian plants. Between 25 per cent and 50 per cent of the factories in the region restrict access to toilets and drinking water during the workday. The same percentage deny workers at least one day off in seven. In more than half of Nike's factories, the report said, employees worked more than 60 hours a week. In up to 25 per cent, workers refusing to do overtime were punished. Wages were also below the legal minimum at up to 25 per cent of factories.

Michael Posner, the executive director of the organization Human Rights First, described the report as 'an important step forward' and praised Nike for its transparency. But he added: 'The facts on the ground suggest there are still enormous problems with these supply chains and factories. . . . What is Nike doing to change the picture and give workers more rights?'

Source: Guardian.co.uk

Service messages derived from pressure group interaction

In addition to changes to products and processes, many organizations have responded to pressure group interaction by incorporating service messages into their product offerings. Think, for example, about the following:

- Tobacco 'health warnings', which were incorporated by some manufacturers ahead of legislation requiring their use.

- 'Safe sex' information supplied with contraceptives.

- Messages on alcohol products promoting 'responsible drinking'.

- Information on packaging regarding its recycling.

QUESTION

Has your organization or industry introduced service messages after pressure group interaction?

Proactive management of unplanned messages

News stories

The first rule of defending an organization is to start with, and stick to, facts as much as possible. Unfortunately, in many situations, facts are missing or incomplete.

Facts put to rest speculation and opinion, and they stop a natural tendency to assume there is more behind an issue or event than meets the eye. However, facts can tell an unfavourable story, a story that an organization does not want to be told. In addition, facts may tell stories that must not be narrated because of personal, political or other confidentiality reasons. PR practitioners often know more than can be said to journalists, and journalists are dedicated to finding out what practitioners cannot say.

PR practitioners are taught that silence is harmful. During a crisis, they are told that individuals or organizations must do something with media calls, skittish investors, unhappy suppliers, fearful employees and grandstanding regulators. But silence is not always harmful.

Silence helps when

- Pressure to speak is not intense. If the public, regulators, media and others are not pushing to get answers, it might work well not to volunteer them.

- When the issue might be a passing one. If an issue arises that is a one-day headline, 'no comment' might suffice.

- When there is nothing one can say. Often the only justifiable expression is confession and remorse.

- When speaking makes the situation worse.

When facts are not readily available, practitioners must use damage control to defend the organization. Damage control is risky and frequently fails when a story is running heavily through news cycles. Public affairs practitioners are masters in handling wild stories because they do it regularly. Damage control is of two kinds – communicating to gain time until the full story is out or communicating to ameliorate a situation.

There are several techniques that PR specialists often use for damage control:

- **Refutation** – Paint a story as false. One attacks the teller of the story, and the story itself, as meaningless, incredible, impossible or illogical.

One must be careful when refuting a story based on partial facts to have enough facts in hand to build a case.

- **Confirmation** – Praise the person and story that favour your side. Note that a story is possible, probable, logical and fitting.

- **Character assassination** – An all-out effort to discredit someone making allegations by going after the person's heritage, education, background, lifestyle or whatever it takes to take away the individual's credibility in the eyes of target audiences. PR practitioners should be wary about using it especially since it drives issues to the lowest common denominator. Character assassination is difficult when defending a weak position, as it shows the organization to be vindictive and nasty.

- **Diversion** – Create a secondary issue that obscures the first issue. Diversion is a dangerous technique, as it is easily discovered for what it is. The media will savage the organization that is caught.

Blogs

Anyone who pays even scant attention to online media has read about blogging. Web logs (blogs) have blossomed from tiny beginnings in the early 1990s into an online publishing event. There are hundreds of thousands of blogs now, most of which are not worth knowing about. On the other hand, some blogs generate news and influence events because their authors are respected as experts.

Blogs are easy to create and cheap to maintain, and there is no skill needed to start and maintain one. Several sources offer easy and inexpensive ways of doing so. However, there is craft in starting and maintaining a readable and useful blog.

Blogs as personal diaries have little application for PR practitioners unless associated with someone with name recognition. For example, a celebrity blog is a great way to reach a fan base. Blogs without a distinct purpose for existence are of less use. On the other hand, companies have shown the way to using blogs productively in reaching customers and others. Blogging is a proven public relations tool that practitioners should know about.

In conventional blogging, anyone can write anything at any time. However, this is not suitable for public relations purposes. In PR, practitioners need to maintain relationships with the key audiences that help their organizations survive and succeed. Second, PR practitioners are spokespersons for others and not for themselves. They do not have the freedom to speak out about company and marketplace issues without checking with those who have direct control over these areas.

Think of a blog as a low-cost and fast publishing tool that can provide an important dimension to an organization in terms of getting news out quickly. Because the diary is available to all at the same time, it is faster to use than media like e-mail and, because it requires no coding expertise to use, it can appear at the speed of thought. One need only type the journal entry and push a button to get it published. In addition, because it has a permanence that Instant Messaging does not have, blogging leaves an accessible trail of ideas, facts and comments into which one can reach to develop a history of an issue, question or challenge without resorting to reconstructing e-mail threads from different places and times.

However, if blogs can be used by an organization or PR professional, they can certainly be used by pressure groups and activists. If you want to find out what the Web is saying about your organization or its products, just go to any popular search engine and type in the name of your organization (or product) and the phrase 'is useless', and see what appears. Part of the role of the PR specialist is now to identify and monitor blogs and message boards that might contain potentially damaging information about the organization or its activities.

INSIGHT

Repak is an industry-funded not-for-profit organization whose aim is to facilitate and increase packaging recycling. In addition to meeting Ireland's recycling target, Repak has a key role in educating businesses and households with national campaigns and sponsorship. There are two distinctive target audiences, consumers and organizations. Repaks' objectives are as follows:

- To increase the recycling message among the younger, more dynamic audience.
- To create an active level of engagement with 18–25-year-olds

- To create a brand image for Repak
- To promote and drive traffic to the Repak website

With the 18–25-year-olds or 'digital natives' it was decided to use digital media to both engage the audience and create a platform for future campaigns. To enable a two-way symmetrical communications, Slattery Communications decided to launch a digital campaign to support the national campaign. They created Repak Bebo page and a Repak blog site targeted at corporate businesses and Repak members.

A 'Repak' skin with logo was developed and links were available to the Repak website, blog site, You Tube page and the carbon calculator that was launched later. The Bebo page was highly interactive in that it had polls, blogs, a whiteboard drawing competition, photos, and a quiz, a video and blog section. In addition, a large network of over 1,000 friends was formed, which ensured that a large number of people were regularly alerted when the site was updated.

With over 5,000 visitors in the first weeks after the launch and with over 1,000 unique friends, the Bebo site was a great success. With Repak struggling to engage with youth post primary and post secondary education, the large uptake of third-level students accessing Bebo allowed Repak to further interact with a demographic that they considered had been neglected.

Source: Ryan and Jones (2009)

Hainsworth (1990) and Meng (1992) – The Issue Life Cycle

The Issue Life Cycle model suggests that any public issue passes through four stages, very much like the product life cycle with which you will be familiar. The four stages are 'potential', 'emerging', 'current and crisis' and 'dormant'. These stages are explained as follows:

1. **Potential issue** – An issue arises when an organization or group attaches significance to a perceived problem (or opportunity) that is a consequence of a developing political/regulatory, economic or social trend. At this point, there is very little definition to the issue, but a group or organization has identified the issue and decides to bring it to the attention of a broader audience.

   An example of this stage in hazards risk management could be the aftermath of a major disaster event where the question is asked by the public, the media or the political leadership 'Why wasn't something done before this event to reduce the terrible impacts of the event?' This question could be more specific if a well-known mitigation or preparedness measure is identified that could have reduced the impact of the event but was not perceived by the questioner to have been undertaken.

2. **Emerging issue** – The emerging issue stage indicates a gradual increase in the level of pressure on the organization to accept the issues. In most cases, this increase is the result of activities by one or more groups as they try to push or legitimize the issue. Media coverage, and through it, increased public awareness and education are critical elements in the development of an issue in this stage.

   Continuing with the hazards risk management example stated in the previous subsection, the local media broadcasts stories and writes articles about individuals impacted by the event who are asking this critical question. The media seek experts in government, academia and the business world to address the question and to provide a broader perspective. The issue, and the demand that responsible parties (i.e. government, community groups, individuals, business community) address the question, grows.

3. **Current and crisis issue** – Mediation brings varying degrees of organization. Positions solidify. Groups begin to seek a resolution to the conflict that is either acceptable to their best interests or at least minimizes potential damage. As these groups work out their viewpoints and objectives and seek to communicate their respective positions, conflict achieves a level of public visibility that is likely to push the issue into the public policy process. In turn, increased public attention motivates influential leaders to become a part of the emerging conflict and pressure mounts on institutional bodies to seek a resolution to the conflict.

In our hazard risk management example, this stage is when a community comes together to address the issue of why something was not done before the event. Political and community leadership becomes involved and public awareness is at its highest level. It is in this stage that alternative solutions are formulated, publicized and discussed. Some kind of action will result from this stage. This action could be punitive for not acting or constructive through implementation of actions to reduce impacts from future events, or both.

4. **Dormant issue** – Once issues receive the attention of public officials and enter the policy process, either through changes to legislation, regulation or corporate policy, efforts to resolve the conflict become protracted and costly. The object of the policy process is the imposition of unconditional constraints on all parties to the conflict – either to their advantage or to their disadvantage. So, once an issue has run the full course of its life cycle, it will reach a height of pressure that forces an organization to accept it unconditionally.

In our example, public policy designed to address the critical question and reduce impacts from future events is developed and implemented. All parties are compelled to comply with this new policy.

> ### QUESTION
>
> How might the various marketing activities discussed earlier be used at each stage of the Issue Life Cycle?

DEVELOPING RELATIONSHIP MARKETING

Transactional marketing

Transactional marketing is marketing aimed at individual transactions (or one-off sales), rather than at creating a long-standing customer relationship. Transactional marketing is most appropriate when marketing relatively low value consumer products, when the product is a commodity, when switching costs are low, when customers prefer single transactions to relationships and when customer involvement in production is low.

When the reverse of all the above is true, as in typical industrial and service markets, then relationship marketing can be more appropriate (see Table 1.1 for the main differences between the two approaches). Most firms should be blending the two approaches to match their portfolio of products and services. Virtually all products have a service component to them, and this service component has been getting larger in recent decades.

Table 1.1 Transactional versus relationship marketing

Transactional marketing	Relationship marketing
■ A focus on single sales or transactions	■ A focus on customer retention and building customer loyalty
■ An emphasis on product features	■ An emphasis on product benefits that are meaningful to the customer
■ Short timescales	■ Long timescales, recognizing that short-term costs may be higher, but so will long-term profits
■ Little emphasis on customer retention	■ An emphasis on high levels of customer service that are possibly tailored to the individual customer
■ Limited customer commitment	■ High customer commitment
■ Moderate customer contact	■ High customer contact, with each contact being used to gain information and build the relationship
■ Quality is essentially the concern of production and no one else	■ Quality is the concern of all, and it is the failure to recognize this that creates minor mistakes, which lead to major problems

Relationship marketing for mutual benefit

Relationship marketing is a form of marketing that emphasizes customer retention and continual satisfaction rather than individual transactions and per-case customer resolution.

Increasingly, marketers are deepening their conviction that closing the sale is only one of the important milestones in an ongoing relationship. Thus, a car dealership is not only interested in selling you a car but servicing it and, in a few years' time, supplying you with a replacement. This is building a relationship between the client, the staff at the local distributorship and the manufacturer's brand. Viewed in this context, the 18,000-mile service is not only seen to be a chance to make a sale (the income from the service) but a marketing opportunity to maintain and develop the relationship.

Thus, the reception team and the motor technicians are involved in building the relationship through their contact with the customer. Another key concept of relationship marketing is that of the 'part-time marketer' (e.g. any customer-facing staff). Much of the relationship building does not take part with the full-time marketers. In supermarkets, the full-time marketers may be comparatively remote. How the shopping experience feels will be greatly affected for better or for worse by the interaction between customers and front-line staff at the checkout and others in customer contact roles – the 'part-time marketers'.

Although relationship marketing is important in consumer marketing, it is critical in B2B marketing. Organizations do not do business with organizations. People in one organization do business with other people in another organization. Thus, a key strength of an advertising agency, for example, is the quality of the relationships between the creative staff and the key personalities in the commissioning organization. It is a very old saying that 'first you make them your friend, and then you make them your customer'.

This often involves many people interacting with many other people in the linking organizations. A network of interacting relationships is formed between the organizations, which then have to be maintained and sustained both internally (internal marketing) and externally. Thus, in considering the marketing action plan, the impact on all the relevant stakeholders is important.

Relationship management focuses on how these relationships may be positively sustained and developed.

Marketing is not seen as a mechanistic set of actions, intellectual cogs in an industry machine, but as an activity that depends on a network of human relationships to support the organization's mission and objectives.

The move to relationship marketing can be seen as the leading edge in developing from a production orientation (any colour you like as long as it is black) to sales (all we need to do is push harder) to developing long-term relationships of positive benefit to both parties. In traditional sales negotiations, you could end up with winner-loser outcomes. In a relationship-marketing context, only creating and sustaining win-win outcomes will nurture and develop the relationship and future profit opportunities.

According to Payne (1995) relationship marketing should extend beyond just the interface with the customer. Instead he suggests six-markets model whereby relationships should be built in the following markets:

1. **Customer markets** – These are the buyers of the final product, and they remain the final goal of marketing activity. To be able to deliver superior customer value in increasingly competitive industries, modern relationship marketing emphasizes the importance of having appropriate relations with other interfaces.

2. **Referral markets** – These are the institutions and individuals who refer the customers to us. This could include banks, agents as well as existing customers. Therefore, cultivating relationships with these intermediaries is critical to getting new customers.

3. **Supplier markets** – Partnerships with suppliers must replace traditional adversarial relations if the firm is to better meet the needs of the final customer. This can include collaboration to improve quality, setting up JIT arrangements or working together in harnessing product innovations. Marketing must sell the new attitudes essential to these supplier partnerships.

4. **Recruitment markets** – To provide good service to customers, it is essential that the firm has good staff. However, in a competitive market the good-calibre staff member also has a choice. Marketing should build up appropriate relationships with the stakeholders in the recruitment markets (agencies, careers advisers, head hunters, etc.), as well as ensure that the corporate image of the firm is appealing to would-be recruits (e.g. through the design of corporate literature and selective sponsorship).

5. **Influence markets** – These are institutions that can influence what customers will purchase. For example an aeroplane manufacturer will need to convince national governments as well as airlines of the safety of its products. Other examples include pressure groups, brokers, analysts, consumer associations, etc. This influence of marketing often occurs under the heading of public relations.

6. **Internal markets** – This has two aspects to it:

   ■ Each internal department is the customer of some and a supplier to the rest. For the firm to operate smoothly it is important that a client service ethos pervades all departments and replaces divisional rivalries and loyalties.

   ■ Each department or division should interpret what it does in terms of how it serves its customer.

Groups

These are relationships between members of a formal or informal group of participants, such as a trade body or chamber of commerce. Such groups form because of a shared interest and shared values and exist for mutual benefit.

Partnerships

Partnership relationships exist between discrete pairs of organizations, such as a customer–supplier relationship or the relationship between franchisor and franchisee.

Partnerships in action

The Y3 collaboration began when Yohji Yamamoto contacted Adidas to ask whether he could produce a customised version of the classic Stan Smith sports shoe. Talks led to a co-branding exercise that now has its own identity, complete with stand-alone outlets. The collection includes trainers, clothing, accessories and swimwear which use the three stripe logo Adidas. The global creative director of Adidas described this partnership as a win-win situation. A sportswear brand that forms this kind of partnership gets the kudos of working with a major design talent, while the designer gains an extra layer of gritty credibility.

(Turngate, 2008)

Strategic alliances

A strategic alliance is a formal relationship formed between two or more parties to pursue a set of agreed-upon goals or to meet a critical business need while remaining independent organizations.

Partners may provide the strategic alliance with resources such as products, distribution channels, manufacturing capability, project funding, capital equipment, knowledge, expertise or intellectual property. The alliance is a co-operation or collaboration that aims for some form of synergy. Each partner hopes that the benefits from the alliance will be greater than those from individual efforts. The alliance often involves technology transfer (access to knowledge and expertise), economic specialization, shared expenses and shared risk.

Alliance in action

The Natural Hydration Council (NHC) was set up by Nestle Waters, Danone waters and Highland Spring to protect the declining bottled water sector. The first consumer campaign 'You ought to drink more water' consisted of a three-week outdoor campaign which focused on three benefits of staying hydrated: keeping gums clean and healthy, maintaining a sharp mind, and improving performance levels during exercise.

Source: Marketing 22.04.09

Networks

Christopher (2005) suggests that the development of supply networks requires organizations to respond to three major challenges:

1. **Collective strategy development** – The organizations in a supply chain must work together, as part of a marketing network, and must develop strategies that are in the best interest of the network, rather than of each individual organization.

2. **Win-win thinking** – The organizations need to 'break free of the often adversarial nature of buyer/supplier relationships' that have existed in the past. While win-win need not mean 50–50, the benefits of improved performance should be shared among the members of the network.

3. **Open communication** – All parties must share information in order for the network to become innovative, flexible and efficient. This includes information about costs, as well as about quality and delivery expectations. Information can no longer be thought of as flowing only 'upstream' in the supply chain.

The development of a successful supply network, that is, one that is able to compete successfully against other supply networks, therefore depends on the creation and maintenance of a relationship between members of that network.

E-relationships

The relationship between any two partners can be supported by the use of IT. Indeed, many organizations form partnerships with customers and other organizations that are entirely 'virtual', in other words, the parties never meet other than electronically.

QUESTION

Consider all the organizations with which you only have a virtual relationship. Online banking? Shopping sites? How do they use the power of IT to develop and secure your relationship with them?

Search engines and commonly visited sites can tailor the way they communicate with you, or even the products and services they offer to you, by reading the history of your relationship.

Customization

The ultimate product or service is the one that is unique to a customer. Customization or tailoring of products and services is now common, particularly in the online community.

INSIGHT

NikeTown London has opened its new design studio NikeiD, which the company claims is the first of its kind in the UK, allowing customers to customize their trainers with the help of a design consultant.

The design studio, which is set over two floors, offers customers the chance to have a hands-on experience in personalizing their sports footwear, pro-clothing and equipment through a one-to-one appointment with a design consultant.

The first floor iD bar allows customers to either customize products using a selection of materials and colours with the assistance of a design consultant, or buy NikeiD exclusive products that have already been customized.

The second floor iD studio offers a more personalized service, with customers being able to have a one-to-one hour-long consultation with a design consultant and choose between five exclusive styles: the Classic BW, Dunk Hi, Dunk Lo, Women's Dunk and Air Max 90.

The unveiling of this London studio follows the opening of a similar studio in New York in early October and comes after pilot NikeiD spaces have been opened in France and Japan.

The opportunity for Nike consumers to customize their trainers is not a new concept. Since NikeiD's inception in 1999, Nike customers have been able to create customizations online by visiting www.nikeid.com, where they can store their design in online 'lockers', share their designs with their friends and order their customized products from the website.

In the same way, once customers have created their designs in the London studio, they will be stored in an online locker. Once they have been ordered, they will either be delivered to the store for the customer to pick up or delivered to the customer's house.

Product prices can vary, with the average range between £65 and £145.

Trevor Edwards, vice-president of brand category management for Nike, said, 'The world has changed. Customers interact with brands on their own terms. The NikeiD studio enables customers to create their expression of the Nike brand with the guidance of a skilled design consultant.'

Source: BrandRepublic

Internal customer relationships

As mentioned above, an internal market has two aspects to it:

- Each internal department is the customer of some and a supplier to the rest. For the firm to operate smoothly it is important that a client service ethos pervades all departments and replaces divisional rivalries and loyalties.

- Each division or department should interpret what it does in terms of how it serves its customer.

Consider your internal customers and how important it is that there is good internal communication in an organization. Think about how sometimes you are the customer and someone else is the service provider.

For example, when you receive your payslip from the finance department, you are the customer and expect it to be correct, to be delivered on time and the salary payment actually credited to your bank account. If there is a problem, you expect to be dealt with courteously and promptly. You do not expect to have to engage in lengthy correspondence to rectify a mistake. If you do receive information from the finance department – say, for example, about a new profit-related pay scheme – you expect it to be clearly written and well presented.

At other times, you could be the service provider to your colleagues or line manager; for instance, when you are asked to find out the costing of producing a sales promotion item as part of a future promotional campaign. Your internal customers will expect you to have completed the task on time, accurately and to present it clearly at the next planning meeting.

So internal marketing is about working together with colleagues and providing them with good service so that, as a team, your organization achieves its goals.

Just as individuals have internal customers, such as colleagues and line managers, that they have to deal with, organizations have internal customers in the form of their staff.

From an organization's perspective, internal communication is vital to internal marketing and the maintenance of employee motivation and company competitiveness. Simple methods of communication can be used to keep staff informed about new products/services, internal restructuring or how well (or not) the organization is doing. In dynamic environments, where firms need to manage change effectively, communication needs to be harnessed to help staff adapt and become familiar to changes in their working environment.

According to Berry and Parasuraman (1992), who are widely credited with recognizing the importance of internal marketing,

> *A service company can be only as good as its people: if they aren't sold, customers won't be either.*

The point here is that most organizations provide at least some level of customer service as part of their product offering, and increasingly it is seen as a way of differentiating products in an overcrowded market. Without a culture of internal marketing and effective internal customer communications, the employees within an organization face the following problems:

- Lack of communication

- Frustration and non-cooperation

- Time-wasting and inefficiency

- Stress and lack of job satisfaction

- Poor quality of work.

All these problems eventually lead to poor service to the external customer, which eventually leads to reduced profit in the long term.

ACTIVITIES

Practice work-based project

Stakeholders and pressure groups

Stakeholders are those persons and organizations that have an interest in the strategy of the organization. Stakeholders normally include shareholders, customers, staff and the local community. As such we can consider them to be people and organizations who have a say in the following :

- What you are to do

- What resources you have

- What you should achieve.

A pressure group is an organized collection of people who seek to influence political decisions and policy, without seeking election to public office. Pressure groups are, or may become, key stakeholders in many businesses.

Role

You have been asked to present a proposal to the Corporate Communications Manager that contains a set of recommendations for improving the way your organization markets itself to pressure groups:

- Undertake an audit of your organization's stakeholders to identify any pressure groups that are, or may become, stakeholders of the organization.

Your audit findings should be included as an appendix to your report (maximum of two A4 pages).

Produce a formal report for your Corporate Communications Manager in which you

- Provide a brief background to your chosen organization, its products/ services, customer base and position in market (two sides of A4 maximum, to be included as an appendix).

- Explain the concept of pressure groups in the context of the organization's stakeholders in achieving their interest, involvement, commitment and loyalty.

- Summarize your audit findings, including production of a stakeholder map and power/interest matrix showing the main pressure group stakeholders.

- Select two pressure groups that you propose to develop a relationship marketing approach with, giving reasons for your choice.

- Explain the benefits to your organization of developing a relationship with those pressure groups.

- Identify a range of marketing activities that could be undertaken, appropriate to each of the chosen pressure groups, that would add value to the relationship.

Notes on practice work-based project

Guidance on tackling the assignment

This assignment is an opportunity to use stakeholder analysis tools in relation to the power and interest of pressure groups and to develop a relationship marketing approach at an operational level. Candidates are to recommend appropriate marketing activities for each of two pressure groups.

Conducting the audit

When undertaking the audit, candidates should use stakeholder mapping techniques and the power/interest matrix in order to establish the stakeholders and their level of power and interest.

The stakeholder audit may be supported by research into the aims and operation of key pressure group stakeholders and consideration of relevant marketing theories and concepts. The stakeholder maps or matrices should be explained and stakeholder position justified. Generic stakeholder maps that reflect no application to the selected organization will not be acceptable. Candidates must demonstrate knowledge and application of stakeholder theory.

The results should be included in the appendices, summarized within the findings of the report and used to justify the recommendations made.

Formal report

Information gathered from the audit should be analysed in relation to the chosen organization and reflect awareness of the key stakeholder issues in an original and innovative manner. Relationship marketing concepts and theories should be appropriately applied to reflect understanding. The marketing activities considered should relate to operational marketing activity, and it is not expected that candidates suggest strategic options. Moreover, candidates should be creative in their suggestions and how they communicate these.

The report should include marketing activities to support long-term relationships with the chosen pressure groups. This should include objectives, targets, tactics and proposed evaluation. Candidates should express their objectives as SMART objectives.

In producing the report, it is important that the candidate adopts a structure and style that naturally lend themselves to reporting on the outcome of their study. The format and approach used will be driven by the relevant themes and emerging issues arising from the research. A formulaic task-based approach should be avoided. The examiners will be looking for a more holistic approach where there is clear evidence of insightful analysis, originality and clarity of expression. The report should be in a professional style with references to conceptual marketing theory included as appropriate.

Further work

- Produce a diagrammatic representation of your organization's supply chain and supply network.

- Produce a comprehensive stakeholder map for your organization.

- Produce a stakeholder power/interest matrix for your organization.

- Apply the Issue Life Cycle model to any public interest issue that has recently affected your organization.

Stakeholder Relationship Marketing

Learning outcomes

Explain the importance of relationship marketing in the context of the organization's stakeholders in achieving stakeholder interest, involvement, commitment and loyalty.

Syllabus Content

2.1 Explain the position and importance of key stakeholders in the market-oriented organization and establish relationship priorities for the organization.

2.2 Explain the concept of relationship marketing and its approach in developing customer retention, encouraging customer loyalty, stakeholder interest and engagement both internally and externally.

2.3 Explain how relationship marketing is based on trust, commitment and cooperation and the importance of this concept not only to customers but the broader stakeholder audience.

2.4 Explain how relationship marketing can contribute to both long-term and short-term customer retention.

KEY STAKEHOLDERS AND RELATIONSHIP PRIORITIES

Stakeholder mapping

The mendelow matrix

In Unit 1, we looked at how stakeholders might be classified according to their power and interest. The Mendelow matrix is shown in Figure 2.1 below.

INSIGHT

When the vacuum cleaner manufacturer Dyson proposed closure of a factory and relocation abroad, the completed matrix for the stakeholder groups looked like the one shown in Figure 2.2.

Scholes (1998) suggests strategies to deal with each quadrant, which are explained in the following sections (with reference back to the Dyson example).

Minimal effort

Box A – direction. This means that their lack of interest and power makes them malleable. They are more likely than others to accept what they are told and follow instructions. Factory management should not reappoint the

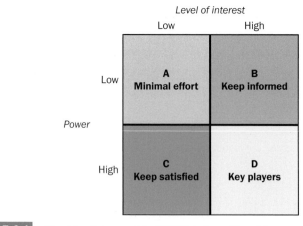

 FIGURE 2.1   *The Mendelow matrix (1991) Aubrey Mendelow.*

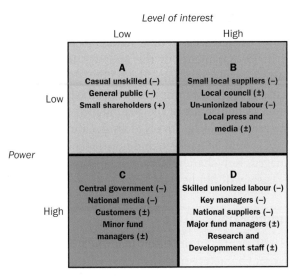

Level of interest

Figure content:

Level of interest — Low / High

Power — Low / High

A
Casual unskilled (–)
General public (–)
Small shareholders (+)

B
Small local suppliers (–)
Local council (±)
Un-unionized labour (–)
Local press and media (±)

C
Central government (–)
National media (–)
Customers (±)
Minor fund managers (±)

D
Skilled unionized labour (–)
Key managers (–)
National suppliers (–)
Major fund managers (±)
Research and Developmment staff (±)

FIGURE 2.2   *Illustration of Mendelow's matrix applied to Dyson.*

casual staff but rather provide limited redundancy support. There is no need to tell the small shareholders or customers.

Keep informed

Box B – education/communication. The positively disposed groups from this quadrant may lob by others to support the strategy. Also if the strategy is presented as rational or inevitable to the dissenters, or a show of consultation gone through, this may stop them joining forces with more powerful dissenters in C and D. Factory management should brief all groups here on the reasonableness of the case for closure and of the provisions being made for the redundant staff. Advance notice will give each more time for adjustment.

Keep involved

Box C – intervention. The key here is to keep the occupants satisfied to avoid them gaining interest and shifting into D. Usually this is done by reassuring them of the likely outcomes of the strategy well in advance. Factory managers should assure the government and suppliers that the closure will result in a more competitive firm that is able to compete world wide. A similar message may reassure investors if it is backed up with a reassuring short-term dividend forecast.

Key players

Box D – participation. These stakeholders can be major drivers of the change and major opponents of the strategy. Initially there should be education/communication to assure them that the change is necessary, followed by discussion of how to implement it. The factory managers should involve the unions in determining the redundancy package or redundancy policy. Key managers should be involved in deciding the basis on which early retirements should be handled and how redeployment or outplacement should be managed. Key shareholders will be consulted throughout to reassure them that costs will not be excessive.

Gummesson – 30 Rs

In 1999, Evert Gummesson identified 30 tangible relationships, each with different characteristics, that exist within and between organizations. Gummesson stressed that the conventional marketing mix must be re-thought to take into account the development of relationship marketing. Further, he stressed that 'both competition and collaboration are essential in a functional market economy'. The relationships identified by Gummesson were grouped under four sub-headings, as follows:

- Classic market relationships
- Special market relationships
- Mega-relationships
- Nano-relationships

These relationships, and their groupings, are examined further in the following sections.

Classic market relationships

The first group of relationships concern the core relationships of the organization with its partners, and are as follows:

R1 The classic dyad – the relationship between supplier and customer

R2 The classic triad – customer–supplier–competitor

R3 The classic network – the supply chain.

Special market relationships

These relationships deal with elements beyond the classical market and cover complexities found both within the organization's supply chain and beyond. Some, but seldom all, of these relationships exist in any organization. They are as follows:

R4   Relationships via full-time and part-time marketers

R5   The service encounter

R6   The many-headed customer and/or many-headed supplier

R7   The relationship with the customer's customer

R8   The distant relationship

R9   The relationship to the dissatisfied customer

R10 The monopoly relationship – the customer or supplier as prisoner

R11 The customer as member

R12 The electronic relationship

R13 Parasocial relationships (to symbols or objects)

R14 The non-commercial relationship

R15 The green relationship

R16 The law-based relationship

R17 The criminal network relationship.

Mega-relationships

These relationships are based on the personal and cultural aspects of the organization and the problems relating to identification of the decision-making unit. They also deal, to a great extent, with imperfections in competition

R18 Personal and social networks

R19 Mega marketing relationships – beyond the marketplace

R20 Alliances that change the nature of the market

R21 The knowledge relationship

R22 Mega-alliances that change the basic nature of marketing

R23 The mass media relationship.

Nano-relationships

These relationships originate, and sometimes operate, within the organization. They are concerned with structure, culture and management:

R24 Market mechanisms brought inside the organization

R25 Internal customer relationships

R26 Quality, particularly between operations and marketing

R27 Internal marketing relationships

R28 The two-dimensional matrix relationships

R29 The relationship with external providers of marketing services

R30 The relationship with owners and financiers.

Factors influencing relationships

Gummesson also identifies 11 factors that influence the 30 relationships:

1. The degree of *collaboration* between the partners

2. The degree of *commitment and dependency* of the partners

3. The degree of *trust, risk and uncertainty* in the relationship

4. The division of *power* between the partners

5. The *longevity* of the relationship

6. The *frequency, regularity and intensity* of the relationship

7. The *closeness or remoteness* of the parties

8. The *formality, informality and openness* of the relationship

9. The *routinization* of the relationship (the procedures that make it work)

10. The *content* of the relationship (i.e. economic or value creation)

11. The *personal and social properties* of the partners.

TravelAffiliate is an Irish-based affiliate programme that helps travel companies to sell their products online through a network of website publishers using a cost per acquisition medium. TraveAffiliate works closely with large travel brands including Gohop, the Irish Hotels Federation, the Star Alliance, ebookers, Tour America, Sunway, the Louis Fiztgerald group and Holidaysonline.

TravelAffiliate provides Irish travel suppliers with an online marketing tool that is cost-effective, measurable and results driven.

Travel suppliers upload their advertising content to the TravelAffiliate system. It could be text links, banner or display links, or even a complete booking engine. Website publishers can select the partners they want to feature on their websites and are rewarded financially whenever a sale is generated through a referral originating from their site, as long as the transaction happens within 30 days of the original click through.

TravelAffiliate is essentially brokering the relationship between advertisers and publishers, and facilitating independent management of those relationships. Suppliers upload their campaign content only once, and TravelAffiliate manages the process of establishing relationships with publishers and assigning unique tracking IDs and all of the administration.

Affiliate has access to metrics on merchant performance including earnings per click, conversions and average approval time. For each ad creative/campaign there are detailed statistics on impressions, click through rates, earnings per click and conversion.

TravelAffliate demonstrated how an effective affiliate marketing programme can offer a clear win-win for suppliers/marketers, online publishers and affiliate networks.

Ryan and Jones (2009)

THE RELATIONSHIP MARKETING CONCEPT

Relationship life cycle model

The customer relationship life cycle (CRL) illustrates how the relationship between an organization and a customer moves through a series of seven stages (see Figure 2.3). In this case, 'customer' can be interpreted as including prospects, customers, client channels, resellers, consumers and alliance partners.

The CRL stages are as follows:

1. **Awareness** – The 'prospect' becomes aware of the organization and its products/services.

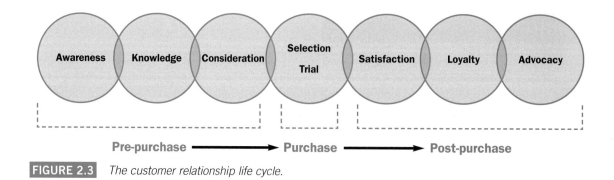

FIGURE 2.3 *The customer relationship life cycle.*

2. **Knowledge** – The prospect gathers information regarding the features and benefits of the product/service.

3. **Consideration** – The prospect goes through a decision-making process, during which a decision is made whether or not to buy.

4. **Selection-trial** – The prospect becomes a customer.

5. **Satisfaction** – The customer is satisfied that the features and benefits did not disappoint.

6. **Loyalty** – The customer re-purchases, or expresses loyalty in some other way (perhaps by telling friends how good the product/service was).

7. **Advocacy** – The customer becomes an active supporter and promoter of the organization and its products/services.

The ladder of loyalty

The model shown in Figure 2.4 is used to describe the development of a business relationship between its customers.

Relationship marketing is used to move customers up the ladder. The essence of relationship marketing is communicating directly with the customers and asking them to respond in a tangible way. It provides the means for the customer to respond and is set up to fulfil the response.

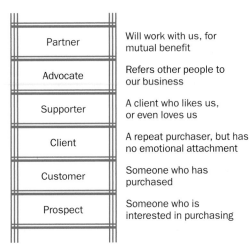

Partner	Will work with us, for mutual benefit
Advocate	Refers other people to our business
Supporter	A client who likes us, or even loves us
Client	A repeat purchaser, but has no emotional attachment
Customer	Someone who has purchased
Prospect	Someone who is interested in purchasing

 FIGURE 2.4   *The ladder of loyalty.*

Developing customer retention and loyalty

There are a number of techniques that can be used to move customers from 'prospect' to 'partner'. The main techniques can be summarized as follows:

- **Customer satisfaction** – In a competitive marketplace, customer satisfaction is the best way to ensure that buyers return repeatedly. To achieve high levels of satisfaction, the effort of all functions within an organization is required. However, there are many cases of companies that have not developed any explicit relationship marketing programme but nevertheless achieve very high levels of customer advocacy.

INSIGHT

The chocolate retailer Thornton's has developed strong loyalty from customers who return to its shops for indulgence and gift purchases of chocolate, despite having no formally stated relationship marketing programme.

Of course, many companies enjoy a high level of repeat business without providing high levels of customer satisfaction. Many customers of train companies may complain about the price and reliability of their train service, but return to it because they have no realistic alternative. Even companies which have an apparently poor standard of service can achieve high levels of repeat business by charging low prices.

INSIGHT

Retail chains such as Aldi and Lidl have developed strong loyalty from price-sensitive customers who consider that the total service offer (access to the store, range of products, cleanliness and friendliness, etc.) is acceptable in return for the price that they have paid.

■ **Adding value to a relationship** – A relationship, to be sustainable, must add value in the eyes of customers. This value can come about in a number of ways, including the following:

1. Making reordering of goods and services easier (for example many hotels record guests' details and preferences so that they do not have to be re-entered each time that a guest checks in).

2. Offering privileges to customers who wish to enter into some type of formal relationship (for example, many retailers hold special preview events for card holders and send a free copy of the store's magazine).

   ❑ Developing an ability to solve problems jointly. For example, a car repair garage may take on board identifying exactly what the problem is that a customer seeks fixing, rather than leaving it to the customer to have to specify the work that they require to be carried out. Such joint problem solving requires a considerable level of trust to be developed between the parties.

■ **Loyalty programmes** – Loyalty programmes work on the basis of providing rewards to customers in return for their continuing patronage. For the customer, a loyalty programme can add to the value of a relationships in the ways described above. For the seller, the main attractions are based on the ability to gather large amounts of information about identifiable individuals, rather than aggregate level data about the 'average' customer. A loyalty programme can also have the effect of 'tying-in' a customer, at least in the short term, while the customer collects sufficient points in order to obtain a reward. For example some coffee shops offer 'buy 10 get the 11th free' and stamp the first two places on the card for free, to build return visits.

- **Creating barriers to exit** – Companies can try to keep their customers by making it difficult for them to defect to a competitor. Suppliers of industrial machinery create ongoing relationships where they are the sole supplier of spare parts or consumable items which the purchaser must buy if they are to continue using their equipment. Many companies negotiate exclusive supply agreements with a supplier in return for a promise of preferential treatment. In both cases, the customer is dependent in the short term. However, such ties can usually be broken eventually (for example when the machinery is replaced or when an exclusive supply contract comes up for renewal), and it is at that point that the true loyalty of a customer is put to the test.

INSIGHT

The Automobile Association (AA) is the largest motoring organization in the UK providing roadside assistance for car breakdowns, financial services, expert knowledge and advice on transport issues to a wide range of stakeholders such as the general public, AA members, government and safety organizations.

The AA currently has approximately 15 active million members and 1.5 million lapsed members but in a strongly competitive market rivals such as the RAC and Green Flag are seeking ways of luring members away, hence customer retention is crucial.

The development of a range of strong relationships with suppliers, business customers and members is important to the AA. The AA is a predominantly business to consumer organization, and it is vital that they receive high levels of customer service and response rates. Customers can choose from four levels of 'Roadside' which provides a minimum level of service, 'Homestart' which provides repair service if a member's car breaks down outside their house, 'Relay' which provides recovery to any UK destination of the members choice if the AA are unable to fix the vehicle, or arrange a local repair within a reasonable time and 'Stay Mobile' which provides alternative travel options.

As a service brand there are two critical points of interaction with customers. Primarily the service provided at the roadside, when the member's car breaks down and secondly when a new or existing members makes a telephone enquiry or reports a breakdown. The high quality of service between the roadside patrols and the AA members has recently resulted in the AA being voted the most trusted automotive brand in a recent Readers Digest survey.

TRUST AND COMMITMENT

The basis of relationship marketing

Relationship marketing creates a new level of social interaction between buyers and sellers. It is based on promises that go beyond the obvious assurances that potential customers expect.

The four dimensions of relationship marketing are bonding, empathy, reciprocity and trust:

1. **Bonding** – Two or more parties must be bonded to each other to develop a long-term relationship; mutual interests or dependencies between the parties must be strong enough to tie them together.

2. **Empathy** – The ability to see situations from the point of view of the other party – another key emotional link in the development of relationships.

3. **Reciprocity** – Every long-term relationship includes some give-and-take between the parties; one makes allowances and grants favours to the other in exchange for the same treatment when its own need arises.

4. **Trust** – Trust is ultimately the glue that holds a relationship together over the long haul. Trust reflects the extent of one party's confidence that it can rely on the other's integrity.

In 1994, Morgan and Hunt developed a model of relationship marketing called the 'Key Mediating Variables' (KMV) model (Figure 2.5). Their model firstly identifies ten forms of relationship marketing, split over four directions:

1. First of all we have to maintain partnership with suppliers (goods and services).

2. Second, we cannot avoid contact with lateral partners (competitors, non-profit institutions and government organizations).

3. Third, we have our 'traditional' partnerships with both kinds of buyers (customer and consumer).

4. Last, the model shows the internal partnerships with business units, departments and employees.

The Key Mediating Variable (KMV) theory then focuses on one party's relationship commitment and trust (Figure 2.6). It is hypothesized that

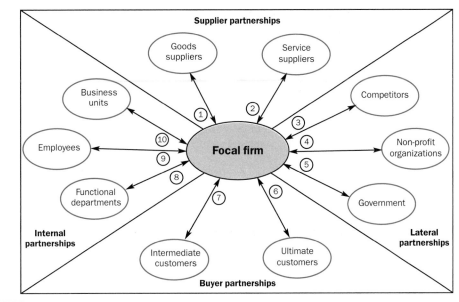

FIGURE 2.5   *Ten relationships (after Morgan and Hunt, 1994).*

relationship commitment and trust are the key contracts between partners to a relationship and positioned as mediating variables between five important influences and five outcomes.

The factors influencing commitment and trust are:

- **Relationship termination costs** – As both parties benefit from a relationship, ending it becomes costly. These costs include the cost of not finding a satisfying relationship, and the actual switching cost in finding a new partner.

- **Relationship benefits** – These include increased profits, improved customer satisfaction and better product performance.

- **Shared values** – These include values, beliefs and policies.

- **Communication** – Of particular importance are the timeliness, quality and frequency of communication between the partners.

- **Opportunistic behaviour** – This is the only destructive influence and includes any Activity where a partner pursues self-interest to the detriment of the relationship.

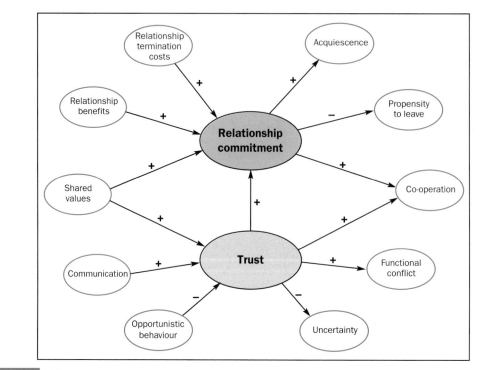

FIGURE 2.6 *The KMV Model (adapted from Morgan and Hunt, 1994).*

The outcomes from commitment and trust are as follows:

- **Acquiescence** – The degree to which a partner accepts or defers to a partner's wishes.

- **Propensity to leave** – The probability that a partner might leave the relationship in the near future.

- **Co-operation** – The degree to which the partners work together towards shared goals.

- **Functional conflict** – The degree to which any conflict is resolved amicably and therefore becomes a positive outcome.

- **Decision-making uncertainty** – The degree to which one partner mistrusts another.

ACTIVITY

Look at the similarities and differences between the factors identified by Morgan and Hunt, and those identified by Gummesson.

FURTHER READING

The soccer club sponsor relationship: identifying the critical success variables for success. – Buhler A., Heffernan T., Hewson P. in International Journal of Sports Marketing and Sponsorship, July 2007.

Service encounter

One of the oldest dyadic relationships in business is between the sales person and the customer. Because it is the sales person who has the greatest contact with the customer during the business-to-business service encounter, the relationship between the sales person and the customer is critical. This is even more important during the time period before the sales person closes the sale.

Social bonding between the sales person and the customer will result in a higher level of customer satisfaction, and a long-term commitment on behalf of both parties to the relationship. This higher level of customer satisfaction can be achieved because social bonding adds value to the relationship in the form of increased service quality.

Berry (1995) discusses how critical it is to market to all employees who may have any contact with customers, so that they will perform well during these encounters. In the business-to-business marketing situation, the relationship between the sales person and the potential customer is the first major step towards closing the sale and developing a long-lasting and mutually beneficial vendor–customer relationship.

The relationship that develops between the sales person and the customer is of particular interest in the area of services marketing. The selling of an intangible product such as a service is usually evidenced by some tangible phenomenon (Kotler and Armstrong, 1994). Therefore, with regard to services marketing, personal interaction itself becomes an important criterion which the customer uses to determine how satisfied they are with the offering, and whether or not they will continue to do business with that service provider. Therefore, how the sales person and the customer bond becomes a critical element in the development of a long-term relationship between the buying and the selling organization.

The service encounter comprises the face-to-face interaction between a customer and a service provider. Selling services is particularly challenging because there is no tangible product available for trial or inspection. The seller must demonstrate expertise about the service and must be credible. In the business-to-business situation, where large sums of money are expended on a purchase, the prospect is faced with the task of buying a 'product' sight unseen (and possibly putting his/her job on the line). If a bond develops between the sales person and the prospective customer, the customer may be more inclined to accept the service that the vendor's representative is offering.

Collaboration

Relationship marketing, like all marketing, is based on the concept of exchange. Whereas in a transactional view of marketing the exchange is of a short duration, in relationship marketing the exchange is enduring. There are a series of transactions that often merge together, and the interactions have a social as well as an economic dimension. The significant benefits of the relationship, to both parties, rely on continued collaboration and an acceptance of compromise.

Transparency

Relationship transparency has been suggested as a potential source of competitive advantage in business markets (Bliemel and Eggert, 1998). Within a transparent business relationship, customers feel well informed about the relevant characteristics of the exchange process and its actors. Relationship transparency delivers value to the customer and contributes to satisfaction as it minimizes the perceived need to constantly search for information and to test the market for better alternatives. Consequently, those vendors who establish superior relationship transparency will gain a competitive advantage.

Creation of value

Evans and Laskin (1994) suggest that the role of relationship marketing is to augment the vendor's core product, that is, to differentiate the organization's total offering to the marketplace and therefore add significant value in the eyes of the customer or consumer. This added value leads to barriers to exit, improved customer satisfaction and loyalty, increased profitability for the vendor and a perception (if not a reality) of higher quality products. Thus, it can be seen that the creation of added value is relevant to both parties in the relationship – the supplier gains profit, and the customer, satisfaction.

Relationship marketing concentrates on long-term, rather than short-term, value creation. A core principle in CRM is customer lifetime value (CLV).

DEFINITION

CLV is generally defined as follows:
The present value of all future profits obtained from a customer over his or her life of relationship with an organization.

CLV is similar to the discounted cash flow approach used in finance. However, there are two key differences. First, CLV is typically defined and estimated at an individual customer level. This allows us to differentiate between customers who are more profitable than others rather than simply examining average profitability. Second, unlike finance, CLV explicitly incorporates the possibility that a customer may defect to competitors in the future.

Note: In the assignment, CLV is only tested at the conceptual level – there will be no calculations. The calculation that follows is included for illustration purposes.

CLV for a customer is, according to Gupta *et al.* (2004),

$$CLV = \sum_{t=0}^{T} \frac{(p_t - c_t) r_t}{(1 + i)^t} - AC$$

where

p_t = price paid by a consumer at time t

c_t = direct cost of servicing the customer at time t

i = discount rate or cost of capital for the firm

r_t = probability of customer repeat buying or being alive at time t

AC = acquisition cost

T = time horizon for estimating CLV

INSIGHT

It might come as a surprise that Johnson & Johnson Vision Care, producers of Acuvue contact lenses, is directing its marketing at 11-year-olds. It is not alone; many companies now identify the 'tweens' (aspiring teenagers aged 9–12 years) as an important customer segment based on Customer Lifetime Value (CLV) calculations.

In the financial services industry, falling birth rates are predicted to lead to a sharp reduction in the number of new customers. Subsequently, there is growing importance being placed on establishing a relationship with young customers (typically teenagers) to garner as much awareness and loyalty as possible.

Source: Cincom

INSIGHT

A new bank account customer costs £20 to 'recruit'. The bank account holder pays bank charges of £100 each year. The cost of maintaining the customer's account is £60 each year. In any given year, the probability of that customer 'defecting' is 20 per cent. The bank operates at a cost of capital of 10 per cent, and assesses CLV over a 10-year period.

The CLV of a bank account customer can be calculated as follows:

Time	Event	Amount	Probability still alive	Expected value	Discount factor	Present value
0	Recruitment cost	−20	1.00	−20.0	1.000	−20
1	Charges less cost	40	0.80	32.0	0.909	29
2	Charges less cost	40	0.64	25.6	0.826	21
3	Charges less cost	40	0.51	20.4	0.751	15
4	Charges less cost	40	0.41	16.4	0.683	11
5	Charges less cost	40	0.33	13.2	0.621	8

Time	Event	Amount	Probability still alive	Expected value	Discount factor	Present value
6	Charges less cost	40	0.26	10.4	0.564	6
7	Charges less cost	40	0.21	8.4	0.467	4
8	Charges less cost	40	0.17	6.8	0.424	3
9	Charges less cost	40	0.13	5.2	0.386	2
10	Charges less cost	40	0.11	4.4	0.350	2
	Lifetime value					81

The CLV of a bank account customer is therefore £81.

Although CLV is an estimate, and can never be 100 per cent accurate, the knowledge it generates should help the organization to create new products and services to match customer profiles, develop appropriate communications channels and construct strategies to aid customer retention and cross-selling. More than this, CLV will force organizations to do the following:

- Consider what drives and impedes customer profitability. What are the major elements of cost and what drives better value?

- Compare different customers. It may be impossible to accurately state the value of different customers, but it is possible to compare their value for activities such as resource allocation.

- Consider different types of customer value and what role each should play in determining the organization's strategy and tactics for managing customer relationships.

RELATIONSHIP MARKETING AND CUSTOMER RETENTION

Superior service and improving the customer experience

Relationship marketing, from the point of view of the supplier–customer dyad, is all about the supplier improving the quality of the customer experience. Although some customers still rate low price as the key factor in determining their satisfaction level, most rank service level more highly. This is increasingly true – as products become more and more similar in terms of their features and benefits, the differentiating factor between them tends to be the level of service accompanying the product.

Improving the level of customer service can be summarized by a seven-step process:

1. Learn all you can about your customers. You will have to find out what your customers' needs are, what they are looking for when it comes to your products/services and what they think about your pricing. Only then you will be able to adjust your business according to their needs.

2. Take time to listen to your customers. Never ignore what a customer has to say, whether it is a suggestion, a complaint or a referral. You actually have to listen, and most of all understand what their opinion is when it comes to your business, products or services. Ask them questions and find out more about their opinions; do not exclusively rely on your intuition. Leave other distracting things and focus on the customers, as they will appreciate your undivided attention and effective listening.

3. Try to be accurate in identifying the needs of your customers. Always remember that your products are not just simple objects for your customers; they represent solutions to their problems and are meant to make them feel better. Be in touch with your customers and, while learning more about their needs, try to anticipate some of their upcoming needs as well.

4. Remember that, in the relationship marketing process as in business, the customer is always right. They need to feel appreciated, therefore build a relationship based on trust by always being honest. If you

make a mistake, apologize. In fact, apologize occasionally even if you do not *think* you made a mistake!

5. Provide your customers with the best support service. No matter what product or service you are selling, a high quality service package is always necessary. Make sure you take the time to explain things thoroughly. Call them, occasionally, to check whether everything is okay.

6. Try to give your customers more than they usually expect. The power of 'delight' can work wonders when it comes to maintaining a customer relationship. Be different from other companies, who only claim to offer more, by actually providing your customers with much more than they paid for.

7. Ask for regular feedback and occasional referrals. When it comes to improving the customer relationship marketing process, asking for feedback is an essential step. Every suggestion about your product or service is valuable for establishing what your customers' opinion about your organization or product really is. Asking for a referral cements the relationship and starts the process of advocacy.

Developing brand loyalty

We saw in Unit 1 that one of the main reasons why loyal customers are important is that they cost far less to service than new customers do to obtain. Developing loyalty to your brand has three key components:

1. Get loyalty early with enormous value. To get attention and have people notice you, do a 'loss leader' in your service. This does not necessarily mean reducing price but it does mean adding extra value to the first purchase experience, to gain that initial business. Let them have a 'wow factor' experience as they get to know you.

2. Consistency is king. Once you have got their attention you cannot let standards slip. You may have done well yesterday, or last week or even last year, but customers only remember their most recent experience. Make sure you continue to add 'wow factor' to the customer experience. And continue to apologize when it is appropriate.

3. Commit to continual renewal. Constantly study new trends in the market. The bad news is that it does not matter what you did before.

You're 'only as good as your last game'. The good news is you can recreate yourself and build brand loyalty anew.

INSIGHT

At Tesco, pregnant women are encouraged to apply for a Club Card and the reward is money-off coupons for baby products. The mother-to-be completes an application form, providing information such as name, address, information about the family and the baby's expected birth date.

The money-off coupons encourage repeat purchase at Tesco's stores. The card means the company can record each customer transaction and establish a customer profile. The company can then target the customer with information about relevant products and services. The organization can also sell this information to other organizations wishing to communicate with customers of a certain age, living in a certain area, who have a particular purchase history.

The Baby Club Card scheme also features a frequent customer contact programme. Mothers are sent magazines with hints and advice to coincide with the various developmental stages that babies go through. So, for example, when the baby is aged four months, the mother is sent a magazine that gives advice on how to wean babies onto solid food and contains advertising and money-off coupons relating to first-stage baby food products.

In this way, both the organization and the customer receive benefits from the relationship that is about timing and delivery!

Stakeholders as advocates

Earlier in this unit we covered the ladder of loyalty. The final 'rungs' of the ladder (advocate and partner) both have the customer 'on our side' – recommending us to friends or colleagues and helping our business grow. This is really the ultimate aim of customer relationship management – having customers who just will not consider ever buying from anyone else and tell everyone they know how great you are.

Profile strategies

Sponsorship

Sponsorship provides a great means of broadening competitive edge by improving a company's image, prestige and credibility by linking to events that the target market finds attractive. Corporate sponsorship has become the fastest growing type of marketing in the UK and United States. Part of this growth can be attributed to the increasing numbers of small and medium-sized businesses involved. Previously, only large businesses could afford to sponsor cause marketing, for instance, as a way of boosting profits as well as establishing goodwill. However, now smaller companies are sponsoring everything from local football and cricket teams to fairs, festivals and clean-ups of parks as an effective method of boosting their visibility in their community. Most of these sponsorships help these companies to enhance their public profile relatively cheaply.

The benefits of sponsorship include the following:

- Gaining visibility in the community

- Differentiating the organization from its competitors

- Helping to develop closer and better relationships with customers, both existing and potential

- Showcasing services and products

- And, of course, increasing short-term and long-term sales.

Sponsorship of events, in particular, can be especially effective as a marketing tool because it can be a means of accessing a wide range of audiences such as decision makers in business, government entities and of course customers. It can be particularly beneficial for companies that take part in international trade, because sponsorship transcends cultural and language barriers.

A growing number of marketers think that corporate sponsorship of events is better than other methods of marketing, as it provides opportunities to gauge customer response to products immediately. Events allow business owners or executives to relate directly with their customers, while they give customers the opportunity to try out the products of a company firsthand. In comparison, marketing research methods such as focus groups are usually costly and may not focus on the right kind of people, while market surveys or questionnaires usually do not allow prospective customers the opportunity to try out products.

Heightened visibility due to positive publicity through the media is another reason corporate sponsorship of events – especially those that attract large numbers of people like popular sports events – can be the most effective marketing tool. Every corporate sponsor seeks the widest exposure possible in both print and electronic media. This publicity increases the visibility of the company's products and services. The various kinds of media that cover the event inevitably include the names, and even pictures, of the sponsors.

Using celebrities

Celebrities get the viewer's attention but whether they work to sell the product depends on proper celebrity casting.

The billions spent per year on celebrity endorsement contracts show that celebrities, like Liz Hurley, Catherine Zeta-Jones, Britney Spears and Tiger Woods play an important role in the advertising industry. For example, Venus Williams (tennis player and Wimbledon championship winner in 2002) has signed a 5-year $40 million contract with sportswear manufacturer Reebok.

Theory and practice prove that the use of celebrities in advertising generates a lot of publicity and attention from the public. The underlying question is 'how can the interest of the public in "the rich and famous" be leveraged by companies to promote their brands and consequently increase sales?' Like advertising, it is no good if the audience remembers the celebrity and forgets the product.

Celebrity endorsements fall into five categories, as outlined in Table 2.1.

These types of celebrity endorsements can be 'clustered' into two broad groups:

Table 2.1	Types of celebrity endorsement

Characteristics of the five types of endorsement

Type	Description	Examples
Testimonial	Celebrity essentially acts as a spokesperson/mouthpiece for the brand	Carol Vorderman/Benecol Ian Botham/Shredded Wheat Ted Moult/Everest
Imported	Celebrity performs a role already well known to the public through TV/film appearances	Neil Morrisey/Homebase Sharon and Tracy (Birds of a feather)/Surf George Cole/Leeds
Invented	Celebrity plays an invented/original role, only seen within advertising	Griff Rhys Jones/Vauxhall Nicholas Lyndhurst/WH Smith Rowan Atkinson/Barclaycard Prunella Scales/Tesco
Observer	Celebrity takes on role of observer, commenting about the brand in question, for example as a customer	Alan Davies/Abbey National Helen Mirren/Virgin
Harnessed	Celebrity's persona is harnessed/wedded to storyline; as such, the character of the celebrity may be evolved through the advertising	Johnny Vaughan/Strongbow Gary Lineker/Walkers Paul Hogan/Fosters

- The first consists of approaches whereby the star's existing and known credentials are 'imposed' on the brand within the advertising context and are potentially influential in terms of the rub-off they have on brand identity. The Testimonial, Imported and Observer roles would all come into this category.

- The second group comprises approaches that are created by, or at the very least integrated within, the advertising campaign. The Harnessed and Invented approaches are examples of starting with the advertising message and building the star into it.

The strong correlation between Gary Lineker and Walkers Crisps backs up research by Audience Selection, conducted as long ago as 1995, that celebrities make memorable advertisements. Furthermore, Lineker's enduring popularity can be linked to his role in the campaign evolving over time to the extent where he perfectly occupies the 'Harnessed' slot.

Similarly, Jamie Oliver's work for Sainsbury's, whilst well documented as a polarizing campaign (40 per cent of consumers in a recent OMD study found it irritating), has clearly benefited the brand by developing Jamie's role beyond the straitjacket of TV chef and providing the retailer with 'foodie' and more 'youthful' values.

QUESTION

Can you list some other celebrity endorsements that fit into the five categories?

ACTIVITIES

Practice work-based project

Relationship marketing

Relationship marketing aims to form and sustain profitably, mutually beneficial relationships by bringing together the organizational stakeholders and resources to deliver the best possible value proposition for the organization. Relationship marketing, through internal marketing, fosters the development of customer orientation, which facilitates market-led responses to change and thus improves competitiveness and positioning.

Role

You have been asked to present a proposal to the Corporate Communications Manager that demonstrates the relevance of relationship marketing concepts to your organization.

Produce a formal report for your Corporate Communications Manager in which you

- Provide a brief background to your chosen organization, its products/services, customer base, position in market (2 sides of A4 maximum, to be included as an appendix).

- Explain the concept of relationship marketing in the context of the organization's stakeholders.

- Explain, and illustrate by application to your organization, each of the following concepts used in relationship marketing:

  1. The customer relationship life cycle

  2. Customer lifetime value

  3. The service encounter

  4. The ladder of loyalty.

Notes on practice work-based project

Guidance on tackling the assignment

This assignment is an opportunity to apply a range of CRM concepts. Candidates are to provide specific examples to relate each concept to their organization.

Formal report

Relationship marketing concepts and theories should be appropriately applied to reflect understanding. The examples given should be backed up with evidence, where appropriate, and candidates should avoid the most obvious or generic examples. Moreover, candidates should be creative in their suggestions and how they communicate these.

In producing the report, it is important that the candidates adopt a structure and style that naturally lends itself to reporting on the outcome of their study. The format and approach used will be driven by the relevant themes and emerging issues arising from the research. A formulaic task-based approach should be avoided. The examiners will be looking for a more holistic approach where there is clear evidence of insightful analysis, originality and clarity of expression. The report should be in a professional style with references to conceptual marketing theory included as appropriate.

Further work

- Apply to your organization, to whatever extent is possible, the frameworks proposed by Gummesson and Morgan & Hunt.

- Discuss the extent to which sponsorship and celebrity endorsement might be used by, and benefit, your organization.

Abel and Cole

Abel & Cole is the UK's largest and fastest growing organic home delivery business and the winner of many awards. They are the holders of the industry's top accolade, Organic Retailer of the Year 2004, National Customer Service Award in 2006, 2007 and 2008.

Abel and Cole deliver organic fruit and vegetable boxes in London and the South East. They offer a wide range of carefully sourced food and drink to a loyal and discerning customer base. Abel and Cole offer weekly selections of seasonal fruit and vegetables, along with a wide range of outstanding British organic meats, sustainably caught sea fish, a complete dairy selection, freshly baked organic breads, organic beers, wines and juices and pantry goods.

Abel and Cole are set apart from the competition by the products and the service they offer. Their fresh produce selections are personalized to each customer's preferences. Their service includes delivery to the doorstep for no extra charge, an automatic shopping system, an extremely friendly telephone service, automatic payment facilities and a news and recipes sheet with every delivery. Abel and Cole also have a fully interactive website where customers can manage their own accounts online 24 hours a day. They have built highly sophisticated IT systems to enable them to provide this efficient and flexible service for their customers.

At the heart of Abel & Cole is the desire to work in partnership with farmers and growers, to serve them as well as the customer. Their relationship with the farmers gives them access to superb quality and variety at good prices, which enables them to give a better service to their customers. They are particularly committed to British farmers though they do source some products such as bananas, coffee and chocolate through the Fairtrade scheme.

Able and Cole give fairs deals to farmers, fundraise with local schools and insist on the highest levels of animal welfare. The Farmer's Choice is their non-profit scheme, which raises over £4000 a week for schools and gets kids eating organic fruit and veg. They donate organic food to Naomi House Children's Hospice in Andover. They help charities lay on Christmas dinners with organic turkeys in Britain. In 2008, they contributed produce and ran workshops with Kids' Company and The Passage – a day centre for the homeless. Any bruised produce that does not make it into the boxes is given to the gorillas, tortoises and monkeys at Longleat Safari in Wiltshire.

Questions

1. Identify Abel and Cole's stakeholders.

2. Assess the stakeholders' impact on Abel and Cole's marketing activities.

3. Explain how e-marketing and direct mail can help develop and maintain effective CRM for Abel and Cole.

Using the Marketing Mix

Learning outcomes

Explain how the marketing mix can be effectively coordinated to support internal and external stakeholder relationships.

Syllabus Content

3.1 Explain how a coordinated marketing mix can be used to meet the needs of an organization's broader stakeholder audience.

3.2 Analyse the behaviour and opinions of the decision-making units in order to design and coordinate a marketing mix that is responsive to stakeholders' needs and adds value to them.

3.3 Explain the dependencies of people, place and process in supporting relationship marketing approaches.

3.4 Explain the methods available for measuring the success of a coordinated marketing mix aimed at multiple stakeholders.

THE COORDINATED MARKETING MIX

Meeting the needs of stakeholders

DEFINITION

Just as a quick reminder . . . Kotler and Lane Keller (2006) define the marketing mix as
The set of controllable variables and their levels that the firm uses to influence the target market.

Why mix marketing?

The manager must address these fundamental areas so that *all 'the Ps' combine* to emphasize marketing as a *total system of coordinated organizational activity* focused on *satisfying customer needs*. For the majority of private sector organizations the aim of marketing is, generally speaking, synonymous with the overall purpose of maximizing financial returns. There are clearly a wide variety of possible *combinations of marketing variables* which management can select. Inevitably some combinations will earn greater financial returns than others. The crucial combination of factors comprising the marketing mix is therefore of high significance.

I have added the emphasis not just to remind you *why* the marketing mix is so important but also to remind you that we normally consider the mix in terms of either *customer needs or organizational objectives*. If we look at the former, then the mix can be targeted, in a fairly simplistic way, at achieving what the customer wants from it. However, if we look at the latter (as we should), then we need to consider the needs of all stakeholders and not just customers.

Conflicting stakeholder needs

The financial needs of a student are different from those of someone buying a house and yet again different from those of the 'grey' market, the retired. A large bank will have all these segments in its customer base and will need to devise appropriate offerings for each of them or lose profitable business. It will also have to consider the needs of shareholders (for profit) and staff (for job satisfaction or a pleasant working environment).

Often the needs of different stakeholder groups are in direct conflict. If customers want the bank to open more branches, but shareholders want costs reduced by encouraging online banking, what are marketers to do?

QUESTION

Assess the different stakeholder conflicts of high street banks closing branches and implementing more online services.

Multiple mixes for different stakeholders

However, it is not just the products that need to be adapted but the whole marketing mix. For example, if we select just one element of the mix, 'Place' (convenience): for the young professional working out of hours, access to services may be key (online banking could be a solution). For the less mobile retired client, local access may be more relevant. This may be the physical presence of a small local branch or possibly online banking as well. However, with online banking, the message to the professional is 'services when you need them' and for the retired 'all your financial services from the comfort of your own home'.

Thus, it is not sufficient to devise a product and then tag on the other elements of the mix as an afterthought. It is the complete mix that is experienced by each customer, and the customer experiences shapes the attitude towards the purchase. Each element of the mix needs detailed consideration whilst ensuring a seamless proposition to the target segments when they are brought together – a totally integrated marketing mix.

Product

The product life cycle

Products do not go on forever; they have a life and go through stages (Figure 3.1): the PLC. In the standard PLC, products go through an introductory phase then, if successful, grow. Here, care must be taken. People can think that growth will continue forever. It does not; the market becomes saturated, and the product enters the maturity phase. The product then declines and may become totally obsolete, unmarketable and unavailable (e.g. by the end of the decade old analogue TVs will no longer work; the only signals that will be available will be digital).

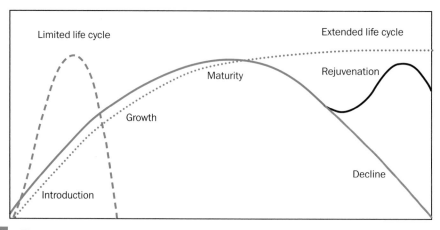

FIGURE 3.1   *The product life cycle.*

INSIGHT

A particular problem faces the manufacturers of classic fragrance brands.

There are fashion trends in fragrances, and younger consumers may find an established classic fragrance not to their taste. However, just changing the existing product could alienate the existing, still loyal users. The solution is to launch a variant but maintain the brand values. 'Poison' now has 'Tender Poison'. Such brands can also be rejuvenated with limited life products available for a restricted period only (e.g. Jean-Paul Gaultier Summer Fragrance).

However, this outcome is not always inevitable. Some products appear to go on forever. Chanel No. 5 is 80 years young and remains among the top ten selling perfumes in the twenty-first century. This is not an accident; Yardley, the original producer of English Lavender, went out of business after over 100 years in the fragrance industry; they had not appropriately rejuvenated the brand. Chanel's success is built on exemplary marketing. The brand, as well as the individual fragrances, is supported at all times.

QUESTION

How would you 'refresh' one of your organization's products or services? What might the critical success factors be?

Different cycles

Every few years, a product is re-launched with contemporary imagery, and it exudes timeless elegance. Some products appear to have an almost infinite life cycle, such as tea. We may switch from loose tealeaves to bags, but we still drink tea. This is in contrast to some other products where the life cycle can be measured in months.

Computer games are an example of a very turbulent market with many new introductions, but by the end of the year today's top game will be in the bargain bin (limited life cycle). Again, the brand may possibly be rejuvenated by the re-launching of a modified product (e.g. Tomb Raider II). Sometimes a product may decline in the major market yet find an extended life cycle in a specialist sector. The traditional vinyl record has predominantly been replaced by digital technology, except in the nightclub, where DJs still find vinyl the medium of choice.

INSIGHT

For the past 25 years, the video cassette recorder has been an indispensable piece of electrical equipment for TV viewers around the globe. However, in early 2005, Britain's largest electrical retailer, Dixons, announced that they would no longer sell video cassette recorders, instead concentrating on DVD players and recorders. A half-century of cathode ray tubes in TVs is rapidly coming to an end with new, flat screen plasma and LCD technologies.

In the UK, digital terrestrial television has already been widely adopted. The government plans to completely phase out old analogue TV transmissions between 2007 and 2012, making most existing UK TV receivers redundant, unless new digital adapters known as a 'set-top box' are used.

The BBC has already demonstrated a high-definition TV service (HDTV) and is considering making it widely available via the emerging digital network.

The PLC and marketing activity

The PLC is a useful concept, but its application needs imaginative use of marketing tools:

- During the introduction phase, competition may be lighter (or even non-existent) if the product is new. The main impact on the marketing mix will be as follows:

  1. Heavy marketing communications will be needed to support the launch, creating awareness.

  2. Communications will need to cover all stages of the AIDA model.

  3. Packaging will have to be designed to not only protect the product but also to carry marketing messages.

4. If the product is not new, the whole marketing mix will have to be very different, as the aim will be to encourage customers to switch from brands to which they are already loyal.

5. Channels of distribution need to be built where they may never have existed before.

6. Dealers should be offered promotional assistance, such as training and incentives, to support the product – a 'push' strategy.

7. Primary demand/pioneering information needs to be developed; communications should stress the benefits of the product to the consumer, as opposed to the brand name of the particular product, since there will be little competition at this stage, and you need to educate consumers of the product's benefits.

8. Price skimming – a high price needs to be set in order to recover developmental costs as soon as possible.

9. Price penetration – a low price has to be set in order to avoid encouraging competitors to enter the market, this also helps increase demand and therefore allows the company to take advantage of economies of scale.

- During market growth, some competition may emerge, but as the market is growing this may not be too damaging. The marketing communications effort may still be high, but as there are higher sales volumes, the product should become profitable. However, cash flow may still be an issue, as with increasing volumes, increased funds will be needed to finance stock and work-in-progress. Strong profits do not always result in a positive cash flow if the business is hungry for new working capital; this is a major problem for young, growing companies. The marketing mix might change to include the following:

1. May need to perform some type of product modification to correct weak or omitted attributes in the product.

2. Need to build brand loyalty (selective demand). Communications should stress the brand of the product; since consumers are more aware of the product benefits, and there is more competition,

communications must differentiate your offering from your competitors'.

3. May begin to move towards intensive distribution – the product is more accepted, therefore intermediaries are more inclined to risk accepting the product.

4. Price dealing/cutting or meeting competition, especially if previously adopted a price skimming strategy.

■ At maturity, there may be more competition, and profit margins may start to come under pressure, but with the stock-build phase complete, little additional working capital will be required, and so the result should be a healthy cash flow:

1. A product may be rejuvenated through a change in the packaging, new models or aesthetic changes.

2. Advertising focuses on differentiating the brand, and sales promotion is aimed at both customer (pull) and reseller (push).

3. Move to more intense distribution.

4. Price dealing/cutting or meeting competition.

■ During the decline phase, there is even more competition, and profit margins may be under even greater pressure. However, if the decline is properly managed (i.e. no obsolete stock write-off), then working capital can be recovered, and there should be some cash freed up to support new products:

1. Marketing activity might be scaled back to allow cash to be diverted to other products.

2. The product may be re-positioned into the introduction stage for a different market segment.

3. Big discounts may be offered to clear inventory.

4. Marketing communications might encourage switching to a replacement product.

QUESTION

How has the iPod changed since it was first launched? Does its development 'fit' with the above process   (excluding decline, assuming there are still iPods when you read this!)?

The development cycle

As products slide into decline, there must be a flow of new products to replace them. Although in this section, we shall, for the sake of convenience, talk about new product development, in reality it is the total mix offering that has to be developed. If we are unable to deliver the product at the right price and communicate the benefits, we do not have a product. It is the total integrated mix that has to be developed.

Kotler's eight-stage new product development process is shown in Figure 3.2. As products go through the screening process, some will be eliminated and so, for every hundred ideas originally considered, only one or two may be finally commercialized. It is important that each stage of the process is conducted as well as possible.

Generating ideas is not cost-free, but the sums are relatively modest. The cost of a failed launch is high. The Persil Power disaster cost more than £100 million when a detergent, which not only washed the clothes but also destroyed them, entered full commercialization.

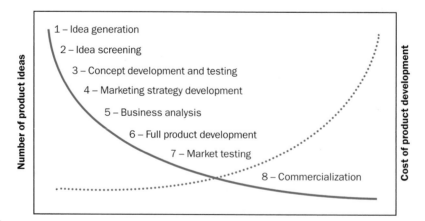

FIGURE 3.2   *Stages in the new product development process.*

1. **Idea generation** – Creative ideas may not be limited to the formal R&D team (and smaller organizations may not have such a thing); the organization should capture ideas from whatever source and evaluate them.

   A key consideration at this stage is not only to estimate the value of the invention but also its protection. Microsoft's market value is not in physical objects but in the ownership of the copyright to computer programs. Increasingly, in post-industrial society, intellectual property (brands, patents, copyright, design rights, etc.) is a key asset. Customers and channel feedback (even customer complaints) can provide insight into how to meet new customers' uses with better products. When all else fails, one can learn from competition. Supermarkets own brands are rarely innovative but good quality 'me-too' cover versions of the brand leaders.

   Innovation is not confined to product but can also apply to process or use. Finding a new way to produce a product, or a new use for an existing product, can lead to a significant change in target market and would require a completely new marketing mix.

   Suppliers can be a great source of new concepts possibly linked with technological development. A manufacturer who develops a super high-speed, high-powered graphics card will work hand in hand with computer games designers to exploit the power of the new capabilities, creating a superb visual experience for the user.

   The continual assessment of the marketing environment can identify an evolving trend and a product hole that needs to be filled with a new offering. Problem solving does not only lead to a product that solves the problem but also generates a platform for other product developments. The Internet was originally conceived as a nuclear attack-resistant communications system but has now evolved into a worldwide information superhighway.

2. **Idea screening** – This is a difficult area with two potential opportunities for error:

   - The first is to invest vast sums of money in new concepts that never achieve market success. Passenger flight in Concorde may have been an interesting engineering triumph, but in the hard light of commercial day it was a total financial disaster.

■ The second error is in the premature rejection of an idea. It was over 10 years from the original idea of the mouse (a Xerox invention) to its first mass commercialization. Only where it is considered that a market need has been identified and that an economically feasible method of production is possible do we have a viable new product concept.

3. **Concept development and testing** – After initial screening, there is a need for significant investment in development. The product has to be realized in prototype form and tested to see if the concept will actually work and that the technical gremlins can be eliminated. This tends to be largely a technical responsibility, but providing the best start for the technical development team necessitates the best possible definition of the tangible benefits. If the technical team is poorly briefed, the wrong product will result.

   For consumer products, a key link with the marketing function will be the joint development of evaluation panels or focus groups (e.g. sensory evaluation of new food products).

4. **Marketing strategy development** – Development is not restricted to the product alone but the full mix.

   This discussion suggests that the development process is sequential and that marketing strategy development can only start when concept testing is completed; this is untrue. All stages may have elements running concurrently.

   One of the key factors in marketing new products is 'time to market'. There is a major advantage in being the first to market (as long as you have got it right!), and in some cases there is an opportunity window; miss it and the product is dead (e.g. the 'Lord of the Rings' game would not have been a hit if it was launched 9 months after the release of the film *Return of the King*).

5. **Business analysis** – In both the business and marketing analyses, the financial viability of the project will be considered, but in the business analysis broader, business issues have to be considered. Many companies no longer make their own products but outsource manufacture to contract manufacturers in low-cost production areas (e.g. for consumer electronics, increasingly China; Wal-Mart, Tesco, etc. do not make a single product). Thus, there is much that must be done in identifying partners and considering logistics for the whole supply chain.

A product launch with no stock does not go far. In the field, new partners may need to be found to distribute the product or, at the very least, existing channels must be trained and made ready for the new product (e.g. point-of-sale material). The effectiveness of the proposed systems must be continually evaluated (will it all work?) and the efficiency considered (if it works, can we ensure that costs are economic?)

6. **Full product development** – Up to this stage, prototypes are likely to have been made in a laboratory. At this stage, products produced by the intended full-scale processes need to be made, ideally by the contractors who will be used in the final commercialization. Then, full beta testing can be conducted.

    In new product development, products can be tested at three levels:

    ■ **Alpha testing** – does the product work in the laboratory?

    ■ **Beta testing** – does it work in the customers' 'in-use' situation?

    ■ **Gamma testing** – does it do what the customer wants?

7. **Market testing** – Given the high cost of failure, the opportunity to fully test the experimental marketing mix is a big advantage. Thus, any minor deficiencies in the intended marketing mix can be remedied before the final, full launch. However, this phase comes with two very heavy costs:

    ■ The first is 'time to market'; if you wish to estimate the likely success of an FMCG you need to run the time-consuming test marketing for long enough to estimate the likely levels of repurchase, thus allowing the maximum time for the second problem to work against you.

    ■ Once you begin test marketing in the public arena, it is no longer possible to maintain commercial secrecy (all of the first six stages should be conducted under full commercial secrecy). Test marketing announces to the entire world, including the competition, what you intend to do. Unless you have good intellectual property protection (e.g. copyright and/or patents), you have declared 'open house' and, in some cases, the competition will be alongside you in the market in weeks rather than months.

Moreover, the competition may affect the original findings if they react strongly to the test launch.

8. **Commercialization** – Here the product is launched with a fully integrated mix. There is only one aspect of the plan that is certain; not all aspects will work as predicted, if for no reason other than it is not possible to predict the likely reaction of the competition.

ACTIVITY

In certain situations, a product that has been through beta and gamma testing may not even need advertising.

Think about the impact of word of mouth on product launches – the Nintendo Wii, for example.

Flexibility and contingency options need, therefore, to be built into the plan. Demand in excess of prediction might sound like good news. However, if there are no contingency plans to increase product availability, the unsatisfied need may let the competition in, and you will have built a platform not for yourself but for your competitors. The product needs a rapid response feedback system with clear lines of management control through this dangerous launch period.

Ethical clothing

In England's early manufacturing industries, including the textile and apparel industries, women and children worked in jobs performed under terrible and intolerable conditions. The British government established a Select Committee of the House of Lords on the Sweating System in 1889 to stop the prevalent working conditions.

Few advocates existed for textile workers. The workers were uneducated and usually unable to read or write. In emerging countries, these same conditions prevail. Several studies indicate that sweatshop conditions prevail when certain conditions exist. These conditions are:

- A large unskilled and unorganized workforce is readily available, which may include children.

- The workforce is desperate for work.

- Management practices take advantage of the workforce.

■ The state or government is either ignorant of the situation, incapable of changing or improving the situation or lacks resources and willingness to intervene.

Poverty and weak economies provide the feeding ground for these types of low-paying jobs in the worse conditions. Workers' fears of losing their only possible income are great factors in maintaining silence and having the impossible workloads placed on them. Children in these countries are considered key economic factors in the available workforce.

In Bangladesh, employees are paid $30 per month, which is the world's lowest wage. These workers live below the poverty line. Corporate investors look to the lowest worker costs, and the Bangladesh government is reluctant to set a minimum liveable wage for their workers.

In South America, Central America and Asia, modern companies have found high levels of workers at very low wages. Companies such as The Gap, Liz Claiborne, Kathie Lee Gifford, Nike and Wal-Mart have been criticized for the goods produced in sweatshop conditions by underpaid workers, especially children.

The National Labour Committee representatives travelled to El Salvador in 1998 to see the local working conditions. In a factory producing Liz Claiborne clothing, they found that workers worked 15-hour days, had only two daily bathroom breaks and substandard working conditions for a wage of 60 cents an hour. The women were always tested for pregnancy and fired if they tested positive for pregnancy. Overtime was enforced and protestors were fired. Jackets selling for $198 were produced at a cost of 84 cents.

Kathleen DesMarteau writes in the 16 August, 2006 issue of *Apparel magazine* 'the green movement made a powerful impact with an abundance of eco-friendly new products.' However, despite a few outstanding companies, the industry as a whole is still behind. CSR practices, beyond the conceptualizing of CSR programmes, have to be implemented and developed with persons to oversee the many facets of co-operation required for CSR.

In a recent YouGov survey commissioned by Marks & Spencer, almost one-third of the respondents reported that they had decided against purchasing an item because they were concerned about where it had come from and what conditions were part of the manufacture. However, we must treat such findings with a dose of scepticism – what answer would you give to a survey that asked you this?

INSIGHT

Appearances can be deceptive. Cotton, for most, seems like an entirely innocuous fabric. Against the sometimes scratchy, man-made fabrics, soft, breathing cotton seems positively natural. It is certainly popular: hardwearing, cool in the summer, warm in the winter, easily dyed and woven. No wonder we have been cultivating it for 7000 years, or that last year we got through 112 million 218 kg bales of the stuff, much of it grown in the United States and China, the world's biggest producer. And yet it is a killer, a sartorial narcotic we need to give up. Cotton, as Don Charney, entrepreneur behind the American Apparel T-shirt company, put it, is 'the nicotine of clothing'.

Or at least inorganic cotton is the kind that constitutes the bulk of what we wear, dry ourselves with and sleep on. This is why American Apparel is one of the many fashion companies, alongside names such as Timberland and Patagonia, and many smaller eco-specialist fashion houses, increasing their use of organic cotton. Some have briefly been there before. But now organic cotton is beginning to appear on the high street too: both Topshop and Oasis have launched capsule collections in organic cotton.

Source: Independent Online

QUESTION

Do Topshop's customers really care about organic cotton, or would price, colour and design sell them a T-shirt?

Smoothies for children

Children's main motivation when choosing food is the taste, with no other consideration approaching this in importance.

Younger children also like their food to be fun, and just under one in three look for free gifts and special offers. A similar number are motivated by added vitamins, and one in four is influenced by their friends' preferences.

Almost half of all older girls look for low calories, as do three in ten older boys. Just over a third of all older children are motivated by added vitamins, and a minority want food that looks fun or has good adverts.

QUESTION

What about the difference between customer and consumer in this marketplace?

The last 2 years have seen a number of changes in the UK children's drinks market, promoting healthier options that also appeal to children:

- Low/no added sugar options: Parents have been choosing low or no added sugar options, particularly for dilutables, for a number of years, as an easy way of cutting their child's sugar intake, driven primarily by concerns about tooth decay. This last year has seen several new and relaunched products in this category, including Ribena Really Light, Juice and Vimto. In the ready-to-drink sector, Robinson's Fruit Shoot is now the number one child drink, offering fruit and no added sugar plus a cool image and pack. Available as part of their Happy Meals, it plays a major role at McDonald's.

- Water: There is a growing number of child brands, particularly with flavoured water, using pack design and characters to boost child suitability and appeal. Water is increasingly offered as an option, in schools and elsewhere. Calypso are addressing the teen market with their Calypso Rapidz brand.

- Fruit smoothies: There is a growing market for smoothies for children, building on from the adult sector. The range of Innocent fruit smoothies for kids was launched in 2008, designed to be delicious, with high fruit content and strictly no additives. A dedicated website gives children the chance to play games and learn 'fruit facts' in a fun way.

- Vending: The controversial area of vending in schools is being tackled by the major suppliers. Companies such as Coca Cola have developed a code of conduct and a range of vending packages, designed to balance competing pressures. They now offer healthy option packages, which include still fruit drinks, diet varieties and water. The Schools Education Trust has carried out research to develop vending options that are healthy but also sell. By secondary school, pupils are no longer a captive audience, and one role of vending is to dissuade pupils from leaving school premises, so the selection needs to be right.

QUESTION

Explain the impact of the 'healthy food in schools' campaign of Jamie Oliver?

INSIGHT

Change4Life is the latest phenomenon of social marketing. Unlike consumer Marketing, social marketing is not about selling products but inspiring people to change their behaviour. It is difficult for health campaigns to create lasting social change because the problems they are expected to tackle are so socially ingrained. There are fundamental challenges for the government in terms of how far they want to be seen to be forcing people to behave one way rather than another. Health campaigners have tried a variety of approaches over the years from the shocking tom-laden imagery of early Aids awareness campaigns to humorous characters such as Sid the Slug demonizing unhealthy behaviour, and empathy. The latest thinking, however, suggests that the best effects are generated by multilayered, multimedia approach, with periodic shifts in tone to keep the message fresh.

Change4Life, by which the UK government will reduce obesity rates to 2000 levels by 2010, epitomizes this multilayered approach. The advert made by Aardman Animations is the tip of the iceberg comprising a variety of initiatives, including retail promotions with food and drink brand partners and schools activities. Those signing up receive healthy living tips. Those who do not will be exposed to subsequent advertising by the Department of Health and its Change4Life partners. One future initiative is 'How Are the Kids?' – a national self-assessment survey designed to help families understand where they are going wrong.

The emphasis of the campaign is to build awareness, invite people to participate by signing up to share experiences and receive further information and finally provide a flow of information to ensure the change model becomes ingrained. It is a model endorsed by Eugenie Harvey, founder of 'We Are What We Do' movement, which encourages people to change the world through small actions.

Source: The Times 17.01.09

INSIGHT

Because of their indulgence properties, smoothies tend to be mainly consumed by adults, yet with issues surrounding healthy alternatives to carbonated drinks, NPD manager at Innocent, Lucy Ede, sees huge potential in targeting kids.

Innocent is to launch the children's range early in 2008 and is working on flavour combinations. While Ede says the drinks are likely to have a sweeter profile to suit children's tastes, they will not just be in the mainstream flavours. Lychee, for example, is one fruit that Innocent is working with for the range. 'Children are quite adventurous,' she says.

ACTIVITY

Innocent were criticized for allowing McDonald's to sell their product. Search the Internet for news stories about this, and similar, cases.

Parallel pricing is where an organization takes a view that in one market it can charge significantly more, with a bigger profit margin, than in another market. In general, the price of designer jeans is higher in the UK than in the United States, even if they have the same cost structure as they are made in the same low-cost production area. The brand owners will argue that they are following free market forces and gaining for their owners the best profits possible. The other view is that the brand is 'price gouging' and exploiting its brand supporters.

An ethical and political minefield surrounds intellectual property. It may take a multinational pharmaceutical company in excess of £1 billion to research, test and bring a product to market (e.g. a new drug for treating AIDS). This investment is risky, and the products that fail must be paid for by the products that eventually succeed. No government agencies undertake this type of risky drug research, and without this vast investment by the private sector, medicine would stagnate. The consequence of this is that the physical cost of producing the drug bears no relation to the sales price, as this has to recover all the vast costs involved in the development and regulatory process.

This is the pharmaceutical company case. Many developing countries in Africa have a significant AIDS problem. These drugs are too expensive for the majority of the affected people who then die as a result. In these circumstances, should less-developed countries allow or disallow the local manufacture and supply of the drugs at cheaper prices? Should the drug companies supply the drugs at actual production costs to less developed countries? Would local production by another company, in contravention of international patent law, cause the whole world trade in intellectual property to collapse? In this context, the issues facing the World Trade Organization (WTO) are far from simple.

There is, in marketing terms, no direct link between value and costs. The cost of production of one additional copy of Microsoft Windows is zero: it is an electronic download with almost no physical costs to Microsoft. Users do see value in the software and are prepared to purchase it. Costs represent the floor below which it is not viable for the organization to sell its products or services. The function of marketing is to drive up the benefits for the customer, to increase perceived value and ensure that the sales systems make the product affordable. Efficient value chain management along the total supply chain to delivery of the product or service to the customer drives down costs.

QUESTION

Lower costs should lead to increased profits all along the supply chain, but do they?

The market for houses provides an interesting platform on which to consider pricing. A roof that does not leak and walls that do not fall down are usually considered useful, but it is not the core benefits that sell the house. Status for a 'celebrity address', ease of access to motorways, the sea view and even availability of schools can all have significant impact on a buyer's perception of value. In this sense, each purchaser represents a micro-segment of one, with their own matrix of benefits and values. The result is an almost free market for the purchase of homes. If houses are in short supply and there are many buyers, then prices will rise. If there are few buyers, in depressed and unfashionable locations, prices will fall.

Economists enjoy building complex models of elasticity of demand – how demand may vary with price. The government employs the best economists and statisticians and is still unable to accurately estimate tax revenue. Therefore, we will set aside the complex equations and big computer approach to get to the practical aspects that are really of interest to marketers.

Elasticity is a real effect. The demand for some products does move with price. This is vividly illustrated by the entry of the low-cost airlines that demonstrated that if you made travel costs low enough you could generate a whole new market. If you lower the price, you can encourage existing customers to buy more and new customers, who could not previously afford the cost, to enter this market. Some products do not have a change in demand when the price changes. If table salt costs £0.01 a kilo, we will not increase our consumption to 10 kilos a week.

Interest rates have for the last few years been at a half-century low, making the finance of large loans more affordable. Shifting patterns of demand have encouraged prices in hot spots to move much faster than inflation, so in some depressed areas, prices have not moved as much, thus illustrating the law of supply and demand. In major cities, certain areas command a premium price, as they are perceived to have 'status'. Other factors can influence the decision, for example, for families with children, a house in the catchment area for a 'good' school may command a premium.

There are some side effects. The large rise in prices has provided the foundation for the purchase of second homes in holiday destination areas forcing prices up and excluding local people from the market (changes in pension rules may still add further fuel to the market for second homes); often these areas have lower wage levels than found in London.

The mortgage sector is a jungle with people being encouraged to take low-start-cost mortgages without much long-term protection in the event of adverse interest rate movements.

The endowment mortgage trap has caused problems for many people, with the linked investment policy not providing the anticipated funds to cover the mortgage. The danger is that short-term incentives might drive a long-term investment issue.

Note: This was written in early 2008, before the nature of the mortgage market changed.

ACTIVITY

Find examples of Government support for first-time buyers, either directly (cheaper finance) or indirectly (by controlling planning regulations).

Competition is a key issue in customers' perception of value. Motorists will travel miles to save a few pence a litre. Where accurate price comparisons can be made, consumers become very price sensitive and shop around. For a major purchase, once a consumer has decided on manufacturer and models, increasingly the next step is not to go to a shop and purchase but complete an Internet search for the best possible price.

The 'dot-com' companies were not wrong in understanding that the Internet is changing purchasing habits. They often got the timescales and the way the market actually developed wrong. People are also now able to make price comparisons across international borders and can see where companies are operating different pricing policies. This is further aided by online price comparison sites that do this on the customer's behalf.

Companies have a dilemma in that different markets have differing perceptions of value and affordability, so differential pricing may be necessary. However, a flexible pricing policy (the company view) may be perceived as price gouging (consumer pressure groups). Internet research provides the consumers with this international price comparison information.

INSIGHT

Airlines provide an example of some key issues in pricing: cost drivers, customer value and elasticity of demand. In 2006, the low-cost airlines were announcing good profits and formulating aggressive expansion plans. At the same time, some major 'traditional' airlines (e.g. Delta in the United States) were in grave financial difficulties:

- **Legacy of the past** – In the mid-twentieth century, many airlines were state-owned enterprises with near monopoly trading conditions, and fares were held at high levels and a complex series of agreements effectively prevented competition. With this level of profitability and strong trade unions, high wage levels and good pension packages were negotiated. Slowly, the world is moving to an 'open sky' policy with free competition, and restrictive pricing has disappeared. The scene was set for the entry of a new business model: the low-cost airline.

- **Traditional airlines inheritance** – As discussed above, with past easy profits, employees expected overmanning, high wages and some of the most generous pension rights in industry. Moreover, these airlines operate a complex network of international flights and feeder hubs. This results in their aircraft waiting on the ground for inter connections to be made.

- **The low-cost airlines challenge** – These airlines had no past history of overmanning and adopted less costly employment packages than the traditional airlines. They could run their operations with much lower labour costs; ruthlessly seeking maximum cost advantage, they cut into 'frills' such as four-course meals, introduced Internet booking (with 'e'-ticketing) and dispensed with individual seat number reservations. If this did not give them a big enough advantage with their 'point' to 'point' strategy they had no need to keep aircraft on the ground to wait for connections and so could keep their aircraft in the air for far longer (aircraft do not earn money sitting on the ground waiting). To reduce prices still further, they often operate from formerly less popular (less expensive) airports, such as Stansted rather than Heathrow in the UK for London. To back this up, they ruthlessly communicated their proposition with aggressive advertising and occasional 'silly' promotional pricing such as '£1 one way'. The result has been a rapid increase in air travel (elasticity of demand effect) enabling the low-cost airlines to fill most of their extra seats. The picture of air travel is going to look very different in 2020.

ACTIVITY

Research the history of BA on the Internet, and look at how BA chose to deal with the threat from low-cost competitors.

Place

Distribution channels

Figure 3.3 shows some patterns of distribution for consumer goods. The blocks represent stages where stock is held. This may be short-term in a distribution centre or longer term for a distributor of imported goods. The arrows represent the physical transport process: in general, taking goods from the stock area, loading the goods, transportation, unloading the goods and storage.

The message is simple: each arrow, each block, represents costs, and unless these costs also add customer value the strategic pricing gap is being eroded. The top distribution layer represents the distribution of an imported product sold through small retail outlets. The next shows the situation typical for a supermarket: manufacturers deliver products to a logistics centre; the assorted products for a given store are loaded into a vehicle

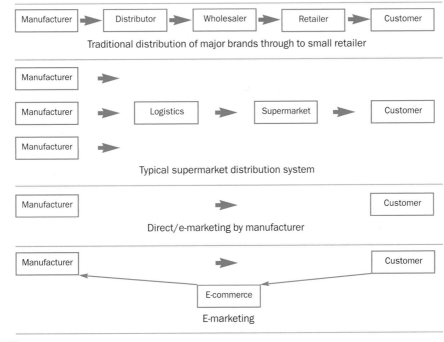

FIGURE 3.3   *Some channel models.*

(a supermarket may have over 10,000 lines but 10,000 vehicles do not arrive each day at every branch) and are delivered to the store. The supermarket system provides a vast array of products at reduced distribution cost. The small independent retailer has a huge mountain to climb to provide sufficient increased customer value to offset their increased costs (hence the death of the village shop/post office).

QUESTION

How does the concept of 'lean supply' fit with this model?

Direct distribution

For appropriate goods (e.g. Dell with computers), the manufacturer can supply the goods direct. Here e-commerce can be seen as nothing totally new; it augments postal and telephone ordering. However, it is much more convenient and 'alive' for the customer, and the transaction costs are much lower.

QUESTION

However, does this also lead to 'shopping around'?

The manufacturer does not need a distribution system; this can be contracted out to one of the specialist operators (e.g. DHL, UPS, etc.). However, this does not provide the customer with a wide range of products, just those made by one manufacturer. Enter the 'dotcom' company; a central 'dot-com' e-commerce company takes the order and, in an ideal world, does not play any part in the manufacture, storage or transport of the goods (e.g. an e-travel company does not own hotels or airlines). Here there is maximum customer satisfaction (armchair shopping with a wide assortment of goods) and efficient delivery with minimum transaction costs.

Of course, the 'trick' is in that single arrow in the e-marketing model. Part of the problem of the 'dot-com' bubble was that people were blinded by the glitz of the capabilities of the new communications channel and forgot the basics: that bargain PlayStation is no use, if it arrives three days after the birthday and is damaged. Even if much of the distribution is conducted by part-time marketers (unlike marketing communications), it is essential to customer satisfaction and it must form an integrated element of the marketing mix.

E-distribution

In the first wave of the dot-com age, only a minority of households had Internet connections, and domestic broadband access was not generally available. Now the majority of UK households have access to the Internet and much of that access is now over high-speed broadband access:

- Weekly supermarket run replaced by Internet ordering and home delivery.

- High-street travel agents are on the decline as more people 'e'-book travel and hotels directly.

- Pirate (illegal) radio stations broadcasting alternative music can now become legal and reach a global audience by podcasting over the Internet.

- New groups can distribute their music by a similar mechanism. They do not have to hope for a big record company to back them. Minority interest music can become freely available.

QUESTION

What role did MySpace play in the rise to fame of Lily Allen?

- How long will the high-street video hire shop last with video on demand over broadband and a large selection of recent films available on a 'pay-per-view' basis?

- Already music charts have a 'download' chart. This may ultimately be the death of the high-street 'record' shop. Moreover, it may change the way artists release material. Now if you only want four tracks from an album, you can choose to download only these tracks rather than buy the whole album.

QUESTION

How and why have sites/applications like Limewire developed?

- Portable sensors monitoring key health parameters (e.g. blood pressure) can communicate to and from a domestic home base using wireless technology (e.g. Bluetooth) and link the patient to the surgery for remote diagnosis.

- Specialist surgery is difficult to provide in lightly populated areas. Experiments are under way with medical robotics. A specialist surgeon in a major city may be able to complete a procedure remotely in a regional small hospital many hundreds of miles away. In part, the 'digital doctor' might replace the 'flying doctor'.

- E-banking is popular with customers (the bank that is always open) and with the banks (vastly reduced costs when compared with services provided at a high-street branch). It is also a really big marketing channel for additional products and services, such as loans, travel money and insurance.

QUESTION

How do these initiatives impact on the stakeholders?

INSIGHT

At the turn of the century, people used traditional cameras with photographic film. When the roll was completely exposed, the file was taken into a collection centre (lots of small shops would act as agents). The films were collected in the late afternoon. The film was processed and prints produced in a central laboratory. The prints were then delivered back to the agent for collection by the customer the next day. Customers could also post their films and receive prints back by post. Technical developments had also allowed the development of mini-laboratories where, at busier collection centres, developing and printing could be done on-site. Prints could be ready for collection in an hour or so. Only a tiny minority of enthusiasts operated darkroom laboratories at home. In 2005, Dixons, a major UK retailer discontinued the sale of film cameras.

As we enter the second decade of the twenty-first century, the majority of mobile phones also have camera capabilities. In the UK, Carphone Warehouse is the largest retailer of cameras. Within a few years, for the majority of non-professional users, the 'film' camera will go the way of the typewriter and be an interesting museum curiosity. Kodak is busy reinventing itself as an 'image realization' company, rather than a manufacturer of film.

With wet film, the need for a dark room and the use of dangerous chemicals deterred the vast majority users from processing at home. Now all computers accept camera memory media and come with image-processing capability bundled in the start-up software package (so much so that the free digital camera is a frequent promotional option). Home processing is now an easy option. Standard colour printers do a fair job (there are problems with long-term colour stability). For people who want to print 'on the move', companies such as Kodak are producing portable photo printers, where the camera or memory card can be 'docked' and images printed. Printing can be slow and media (photo-quality paper and cartridges) is surprisingly expensive.

A second option is the reinvention of the mini-photographic laboratory. Here people can plug in their memory media and print out on higher quality printers with better overall quality and lower print costs for longer print runs. For more specialist printing (e.g. large sizes such as A1) and specialist media such as your own customized mouse mat, the services of the more specialist laboratory are still needed. However, with broadband access, people can send their files over the Internet; there is no need to go to the shop to hand over your film. The finished articles can then be returned by courier service or by post.

The new technology has changed the balance of outlet options for the consumer. Home processing is a realistic option. The mini-laboratories and central laboratories have had to rethink their distribution and business processes (for the central laboratory, inbound logistics become broadband delivery of files, rather than a van delivering rolls of film). The process of a local agent collecting films and customers having to return to collect their prints a day later is a non-starter. The agents appear to be out of the loop completely. Digital processes and e-communications are rewriting distribution of 'goods' and services. A similar revolution will be taking place in the distribution of film and music. Why should we trek into town or wait for snail mail to deliver a CD or DVD when we can download over broadband?

Promotion

The promotion mix

The segmentation process identifies the target segments, and this profile gives an insight into how the mix proposition should be formulated (i.e. the offer that is designed for that segment). The corporate and brand values are an important foundation in reducing risk and building value. Therefore, many organizations will have a powerful and ongoing communications programme to sustain this; alongside the programme are an integrated set of sub-communications plans to support a given project (see Figure 3.4). This is key for the front-line marketer, since checking conformance to house style is an important aspect of their day-to-day activities and responsibilities.

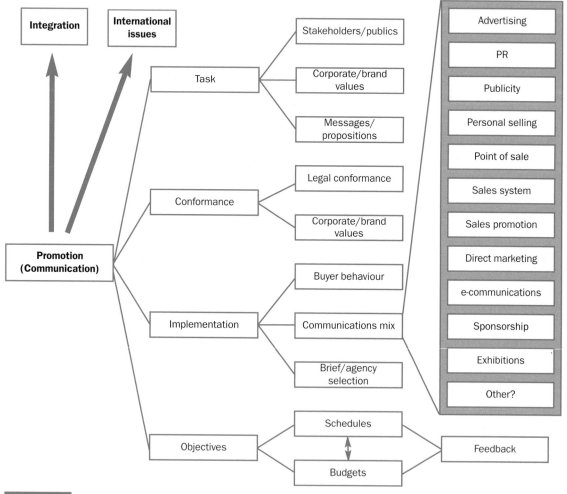

FIGURE 3.4 *The marketing communication system.*

There is nothing worse than finding you have 10,000 brochures with last year's logo in the wrong Pantone colour!

In the section on relationship marketing, we noted that it is not just customers we have to communicate with but all relevant stakeholders. Therefore for a consumer product, the best advertising campaign (pull element of the strategy) is a waste of time if the B2B marketing to the channels has not succeeded in getting the product onto the shelf (the push element of the strategy). Channel staff also have to be trained and incentivized, if we want them to sell the product. Sometimes in the literature on communications, stakeholders may be referred to as public or audiences. We need to define what the corporate and brand values are before we get to the details. These set the tone and atmosphere of all policies and activities. It will then be possible to set the messages and propositions.

The first stage of communications activities is to verify the stakeholder analysis to ensure that it is complete and does not need revising or updating. The profiling process should not be reserved for the customers alone, but for all the stakeholders, so that we can understand their agendas (in American terms 'where they are coming from'). You can see how critical it is that communications intended for one audience (stakeholder group) may be received by another with a different agenda, who will put a completely different 'spin' on the message.

Bluetooth

In a recent article, Brand Republic reports that Coke has some new vending machine ideas on trial in Dublin that use Bluetooth to deliver the content. No, we're not talking about delivering cans of Coke via Bluetooth but digital content.

The Urban Digital Vending (UDV) system can be used to deliver all manner of digital content including simple things like ringtones and screen savers – but less obvious things like coupons, WiFi access codes, and other digital content. They even have a jukebox solution with access to over 2M tracks for download – all appropriately set up with Digital Rights Management (DRM). Not only can these machines be used to deliver content, but the UDV can be used for marketing and self-promotion via Bluetooth rather than just content delivery.

What was unique about this solution is that the consumer absolutely wants to talk to the UDV and the UDV wants to talk to one and only one consumer (the one who just paid money for the content), so getting the communication right is of paramount importance to both parties in the transaction. How does the UDV do that?

The UDV includes a touch screen display allowing the consumer to register their device. The registration process is a simple scan by the UDV and then a display of Bluetooth devices that it finds. If there is more than one device it asks, 'Is this you?' allowing you to confirm that the device has been identified correctly. This simple confirmation turns it from 'opt-out' spam to 'opt-in' targeted promotion and increases its power by a factor often.

Further examples of the use of Bluetooth include the following:

- Marketing targeted at men in clothes stores in India. Get them to play games while they shop. As they play and win, they get discounts.

- Football clubs using Bluetooth to market to fans in the UK. Free content and downloads for fans at the games.

- In the UK, posters that are 'active'. Particularly interesting as it is a local authority behind this (as opposed to a mega brand or marketing company).

ACTIVITY

Assess the marketing implications of Nike and the Bluetooth chip in a running shoe.

Bluetooth is inherently local. There are some good angles to use Bluetooth to promote contextually relevant offers and information. By definition, when you connect to a Bluetooth service, to some extent, that service 'knows' where you are ('in train station', 'in football stadium', 'in store') and can impute some things about what you are doing, or what you might be interested in. The benefits for marketing and promotion are obvious.

Compliance with regulation

As with all company activities the law must be observed. Even within Europe, there are very significant differences as to what methods of communication may be appropriate for given products in specific areas. Highly sensitive areas include communications to children or promotion of sensitive products, such as alcohol, tobacco or contraceptives. This does apply not only to advertisements placed by the marketing department but also to the activities of all people associated with the product and any aspect of the extended mix. Data protection legislation must be observed in the use of address lists for direct mail and so on.

Often developments outstrip legislation or move into areas where issues, for example public perception of good taste, are involved. Here industry tends to practise self-regulation with bodies such as the Advertising Standards Authority (UK) to arbitrate. This is desirable, as the law tends to control historical issues, whereas technology and society's values are rapidly changing. A sensitive responsive system is required rather than the dead hand of bureaucrats.

Examples of self-regulation include the following:

- Football clubs that are sponsored by drinks producers have removed the names of sponsors from replica kit sold to children.

- Television companies have restricted (or even banned) the promotion of foods that are high in fats, sugar or salt (HFSS) between programmes aimed at children.

ACTIVITY

Research advertisements that have been 'pulled' as a result of pressure group action and explain the implications of their actions.

Ethical promotion

Promotion is about communication, a subjective area that is very sensitive to people's culture and social values. Therefore, in one country it may be acceptable to show a naked body in advertising a luxury bath product, whereas in another social context such an image would be outrageous and cause great offence.

In the not-for-profit sectors, the limits of social acceptability are stretched. Thus, in a drink driving campaign violent, disturbing imagery may be used but is only considered socially acceptable given the seriousness of the issue. However, just because the objective is considered to be good, it does not imply that the marketer has free licence to use any imagery he or she may choose. A hard-hitting campaign from a charity wishing to increase awareness and social concern about child abuse depicted an image of a child with a cockroach leaving its mouth. This image was considered unacceptable, and this element of the campaign was withdrawn.

Apart from the imagery, the tactics and targets for communications may cause ethical controversy. Is 'pester power' (the communication of messages to children) a legitimate form of a 'pull' strategy for a computer game or is it exploiting people too young to be exposed to such pressures and messages? In the past, the tobacco companies claimed that advertising of these products was aimed at brand switching and did not induce young people to start smoking or that smoking was an essential part of the 'high life'.

Similar dilemmas face the advertisers of alcoholic drinks. Most recently, the medical authorities have become concerned about risks of premature death from unhealthy eating habits and the heavy promotion of so-called 'junk' food. Again, some advertisers claim that such advertisements just support the brand and do not induce over-consumption.

INSIGHT

At the start of 2006, a hot issue in the UK was whether smoking should be allowed in enclosed public places. There is an accumulating body of evidence linking passive smoking (inhalation of other people's smoke by non-smokers) to respiratory diseases in workers subjected to smoky environments. Two ethical issues associated with tobacco products are as follows:

■ **The right to chose** – Should the state in a free society stop people doing things that could damage their health? People engage in other activities (e.g. mountain climbing) which carry an element of risk and society accepts this.

■ **The marketers' dilemma** – One view is that if something is legal then the marketers should be free to promote the product. The alternative view is that marketers as professionals should exercise social responsibility and not promote products that cause disease. It is of the nature of ethical issues that different people and organizations may have opposing views.

People

Recruitment

If a good meal depends on the purchase of good ingredients, the future of a company depends on recruiting good people. Too often, this is seen as a simple selection process. In taking an RM view, we can see that potential job applicants are a key stakeholder group. We want the best applicants.

Increasingly in the post-industrial society, there are not enough people with key skills. Therefore, selection starts with having an organization that able people will want to work in. If we take a marketing view of employment, it is a free exchange process of mutual benefit to both parties (the RM principle that only win-win relationships work in the long run). A clear specification for the role and person needs to be drawn up not only in hard terms (e.g. qualifications, professional memberships) but also in softer areas such as personality (one view is 'hire for attitude, train for performance'). Customer service is as much about values as skills. The organization also needs to be aware that recruitment channels are marketing channels. Candidates have to be 'sold' on the organization, as well as the other way round.

QUESTION

More and more candidates are looking for organizations that offer a positive 'work-life balance' to employees. Can you think of any other examples of other things that candidates might look for in a prospective employer?

Relationship marketing applies to the internal stakeholders. Retention is critical; poor management will only encourage good staff to move. Replacement and subsequent training of the new staff are expensive. In knowledge-based industries, such as an advertising agency, the greatest asset the organization really has is the creative talents and professionalism of its staff.

INSIGHT

Staff can also be advocates for the business. Lloyds TSB considers all its staff (who are also customers) to be a valuable advocacy asset.

Working conditions

Global competition puts pressure on companies. One way to compete effectively is to focus on core activities and outsource the rest. So the business sticks to the knitting. It does what it does best: it produces the items in which it has a competitive advantage.

Anything it needs that it does not produce cheaply itself, it buys from other companies. This is what is meant by focus: concentrating on the areas of greatest expertise within the company.

The business that concentrates on its core capabilities may require a great many suppliers. These need to be organized in a complex supply chain that is carefully coordinated. The businesses that participate will become interdependent. For each, future success will require continuing good relationships with each other.

It is now common for services as well as manufacturing businesses to outsource. For example, many banks like Barclays have outsourced their call centres to places like India, as they can save up to 60 per cent of their running costs. Wages and rent are both lower. They have taken advantage of advances in technology.

There are big issues here relating to security of employment and fair pay. Also, organizations can have major problems with conflicting cultures between countries.

Flexibility is an essential source of competitive advantage for businesses. Offshoring allows organizations to reduce activity levels without losing their own staff.

QUESTION

Is this approach ethical? Do customers care? How do staff feel, being asked to train their own replacements?

Competition has brought improved real incomes for huge numbers of people all over the world. It remains the case that for many people, employment security has got worse rather than better. Yet the development of manufacturing and services in the poorer countries of the world has brought massive improvements in standards of living for the people who work there.

INSIGHT

As an alternative to subcontracting globally, some businesses are behaving in an altogether different way. One such business is Intel, the computer chip business. Here global management is driven by technological change. The Intranet and Internet, teleconferencing, instant messenger, 90,000 laptops and wireless connections allow its employees to stay in touch with each other in any country whether in the office or not. This, combined with emerging labour markets, allows Intel to employ the best wherever they live in the world. It also means Intel as a company never sleeps as it has employees in different time zones. E-mails and teleconference meetings are 24/7.

Intel can organize virtual teams across the world. For example, marketing specialists in the UK can communicate with the best designers, who may happen to be in Russia. Work is something you do, not some place you go. No need to outsource and you have more control. Intel has 90,000 employees in 45 countries operating globally and staying within its core activity.

QUESTION

Earlier we looked at the issues surrounding the ethical production of clothing and at allegations of the use of 'sweatshop' production in less developed countries. Do you think customers care about an organization's working conditions? Are their concerns translated into purchasing activity?

The European Union adopted a Charter of Fundamental Social Rights at Strasbourg in 1989. A Social Action programme was set up to implement the Social Charter.

The Charter guarantees a range of basic rights for workers in the EU. These include the following:

- A minimum wage

- A maximum working week

- A minimum paid holiday

- Improved maternity and paternity leave

- Access to training

- The right to be informed and consulted regarding major company decisions.

In 1992, the Social Charter was incorporated into the Social Chapter of the Maastrict Treaty, the agreement that set up the single market. The theory was that the single market provided an opportunity for member countries to trade with one another freely and on equal terms. This meant that all companies operating in the EU would be providing similar working conditions and would therefore have similar cost structures.

All the EU member countries except the UK agreed to the Social Charter. The UK's reservations centred on the views of many business managers, which were put forward by bodies such as the Confederation of British Industry (CBI) and the Institute of Directors.

They thought that the moves towards employee participation would raise costs and reduce their authority. They were also against improvement in working conditions, as these would also raise costs.

As a consequence the UK government negotiated an 'opt out' clause. This allowed it to agree to everything in the Maastrict Treaty except the social provisions.

In 1997, the new Labour government agreed to the Social Chapter. Many large businesses had already been implementing the provisions and were happy with the outcome. Some businesses are still worried.

For example, paid maternity leave was extended from six to nine months from 2007 and the burden of improved parental rights fell heavily on small businesses that happened to employ a higher percentage of young female staff.

ACTIVITY

How would you communicate an organization's stance on working conditions and employee treatment to stakeholders? Make notes about the impact of such an initiative on other areas of the marketing mix.

Other modern management approaches also impact on different stakeholder groups. These include the following:

- Working from home

- Flexi-time

- Hot desking (perhaps to reduce costs or even carbon footprint).

QUESTION

Which stakeholders might be concerned about initiatives such as these?

Equal opportunities

The 1970 Equal Pay Act was introduced to end discrimination between men and women. It was amended in 1984 to enable men and women to claim equal wages for work of equal value done for the same employer or an associated employer.

The Sex Discrimination Acts 1975 and 1986 declare that it is unlawful to be less favourably treated because of your sex or because you are married.

Despite legislative protection, female employees remain at a real relative disadvantage. The principle of equal pay for equal work is often very difficult to ensure or to enforce. In addition, female employees are much more likely to occupy temporary or part-time posts, which carry much reduced rights and low status. The Social Chapter may address this issue.

The Race Relations Act 1976 outlaws all racial discrimination. It also established the Commission for Racial Equality, which has direct responsibility for monitoring the effect of the Act. Despite the existence of the law, it is clear that discrimination still occurs; being a member of a racial minority reduces market power. The outcome is visible not so much in terms of lower pay as in higher unemployment.

Recent research shows that ethnic minorities still face disadvantages. Not only are their rates of pay below average, but they may experience all kinds of hidden or open discrimination when making applications for employment. Most companies claim to operate without any racial discrimination, but they cannot alter attitudes among their own personnel, who may penalize members of ethnic minorities in ways that are difficult to expose or to eradicate. The same problems can arise for people who are disabled or who are known to be homosexuals.

The experience of negative discrimination is often humiliating and deeply frustrating. As well as any legal obligations, employers have a responsibility to ensure that everyone in the firm enjoys full respect and proper rights with fair rewards and prospects.

Firms can also be argued to have a wider social and ethical duty to offer opportunities to all sectors of the community. Hiring the best person for the job should be the most effective strategy. Businesses that have made progress in creating equal opportunities often believe in it as a way of improving performance. However, some are criticized for 'just trying to balance the numbers', rather than hiring candidates on merit.

QUESTION

Think how you could incorporate information about the organization's equal opportunities stance into its marketing communications. Would you do it in a direct way, by making a clear statement, or indirectly, by showing a diverse mix of staff and customers in advertisements and literature? Might stakeholders see the use of 'diverse publics' in marketing literature as condescending?

Process

Tailoring processes to stakeholders

Marketing is, essentially, about increasing revenues and profits. Customers are no longer just interested in what the product is; they also 'care' about how it is produced. Shareholders might prefer to invest in organizations with a clear ethical and corporate social responsibility (CSR) stance. Employees, too, are increasingly concerned that the organization with which they are associated should be seen as 'caring' and might use CSR as a key decision criterion when seeking employment. CSR can also motivate staff. CSR is dealt with in more detail in Unit 4 of this text.

Recycling

Many stakeholders, perhaps prompted by government initiatives such as the Kyoto summit and 'green bin' recycling issues, are now concerned about the environmental impact of production processes.

QUESTION

The purpose of packaging is

- To protect the product

- To facilitate distribution

- To carry product information, some of which may be required by law

- To carry marketing communications.

Is that it? What about the trade-off between all of the above and the desire of consumers and other stakeholders for less packaging and recyclability?

Service organizations are not immune from arguments about recycling:

- The concept of 'the paperless office', where processes are automated and communications (and document archiving) are electronic, should reduce the amount of paper created within the organization.

- The segregation of waste in the office, by means of 'multiple bin' schemes, should ensure that essential paper can be recycled.

- The growth in e-marketing should reduce the volume of 'junk mail' produced by marketing departments to end its life (unread) in landfill.

QUESTION

Has the 'paperless office' really happened? Statistics suggest that paper use at work has trebled since the invention of the PC!

Despite these 'modern' approaches to business, most organizations still have a long way to go if they want to minimize their environmental impact.

Alternative energy

INSIGHT

With the globe facing the ever-growing threat of climate change, Olympic chiefs are increasingly worried about the environmental damage caused by the Olympic flame.

Now, in an effort to ensure London's 2012 Olympics are remembered as the 'greenest' ever, organizers are exploring ways of developing a more carbon neutral flame which will be kept alight in a cauldron in the main stadium for the month of Olympic and Paralympic competition.

A spokeswoman for London 2012 said: 'We want London 2012 to be a truly sustainable Games. Using a low-carbon fuel to light the Olympic flame and keep it burning throughout the Games is one of the many things we are looking at right now to deliver a "green games" '.

'The Olympic games and Paralympic games have the power to set agendas, and change behaviour, and applying sustainability principles to one of the most potent symbols of the Games will, we hope, help us do just that.'

To that end, London 2012 are now in talks with one of their major sponsors, the French company EDF, about finding an energy source which will reduce carbon emissions.

Source: The Telegraph Online

QUESTION

How could your organization benefit, in marketing terms, from a reduced 'carbon footprint'? How would you tell your stakeholders?

Food miles

Having been through a period of growth in organic products, during the 1990s, the latest area of concern for food retailers is that of 'food miles'. What this concept means is minimizing the distance food has travelled, from producer to customer, and favouring 'local' (to the consumer) products.

INSIGHT

The greenhouse gas emissions caused by baked beans have amused schoolboys for decades. Now they are proving a headache for experts at Oxford University. Last week Tesco announced it would introduce labels on its products, detailing their carbon footprint. The information, it said, would go beyond the mere question of food miles – how far the produce has been transported – to include indirect greenhouse emissions given off during its production and processing. Tesco freely admitted that it does not know how to measure this yet and has effectively outsourced the problem to scientists at Oxford's Environmental Change Institute, along with the promise of £5 million funding to help them along.

The problem for Tesco's grand announcement is that Brenda Boardman, who leads the institute, is in the dark too. 'I don't know how we'll do this either yet. We haven't started and it's not going to be an easy project,' she says. 'Some ways of doing it are contested and there are accuracy issues. The first stage of the Tesco project is to get people together to talk about whether there is a standard way we can do it.'

Source: The Guardian, 25 January 2007

The critical Question, however, is the extent to which interested consumers turn their expressed interest into actual purchasing habits, in that even where consumers have concerns about 'conventionally' produced food, their support for alternatives is usually conditional and often determined by price or availability issues.

Practice shows that most of the ethical labelling initiatives like organic food, products free from child labour, legally logged wood and fair-trade products often have market shares of less than 1 per cent (MacGillivray, 2000). This is at least partly due to the attitude–behaviour gap: attitudes alone are often a poor predictor of marketplace behaviour.

Only a small proportion of consumers are taking ethical labels into account when purchasing. In the case of ethical products, the most important reason to explain the difference between attitude and behaviour can be that the ethical criterion is just not taken into account at the point of purchase and that respondents give socially desirable answers to questionnaires. Another potential explanation is that price, quality, convenience and brand familiarity are still the most important decision factors, while ethical factors are only taken into account by a minority of consumers.

Although consumer interest in sustainable products may be growing, sustainable food markets remain niche markets attracting consumers with a specific profile. In general, the ethical consumer is a middle-aged person with a higher income, who is above-average educated, with a prestigious occupation and who is well informed. For the time being, this market segment is still small.

Physical environment

Accessibility

There are around 10 million disabled people in the UK. In business you are legally required not to discriminate against disabled people who

- Use your products and services

- Are employed by you

- Apply for employment.

This means, for example, that:

- Packaging should be designed in such a way that it is easy to open.

- Entrances and stairways should be accessible by wheelchair.

- Specific facilities must be provided for disabled staff and customers.

- Recruitment practices must not discriminate.

Decor, corporate image and livery

While these aspects of product and service delivery are important to customers, they also impact on other stakeholders:

- Employees need to have the right tools to do the job, but the environment in which they work affects their state of mind and motivation levels. Staff who feel that they work in a professional and well-presented organization, are more motivated and therefore more productive. They will also have a positive outlook, and this will impact on the 'people' aspects of the marketing mix.

- Shareholders need to feel that they have invested in a well-managed, professionally run organization. They will see the 'public face' of the organization as evidence of this. Every aspect of service delivery, from the 'shopfront' to the uniform and the delivery trucks, will serve to further reinforce the fact that shareholders have invested wisely (or not!).

INSIGHT

With their reputations in tatters, banks are having to fight to convince consumers of their trustworthiness, their dependability and solidarity. So it is that in a world of decentralized, contact-centre driven customer service, the high street branch and face-to-face communications have become again the focus of many banks' investments in branding and design.

Barclays – In 2008 Barclays unveiled its 'brand concept' branch design. This features interactive technologies, such as Microsoft Surface tables, that allow users to navigate information on Barclays Premier services through touch, and an interactive Being: London video wall, which displays graphics of information drawn from blogs and customers. The three-floor branch, which also offers specialist areas and private rooms for Personal, Premier, Mortgage and Local Business customers.

HSBC has embarked on a global redesign of its retail branches, with its UK locations leading the way. In the past 4 years, the branches have been reconfigured, so that the traditional ratio of 20 per cent customer space to 80 per cent administrative space has been inverted. Automation has increased, as has the use of express banking, which moves customers away from cashiers. 'Branches are now friendlier and less austere, but we have to make sure the design is sobre,' says Richard Newland, HSBC's head of retail design. 'We don't want a fun palace of a bank. Previously, banks were there to protect your money and be impressive. Now, people come in to talk about options an get advice.'

Bank brands need to be seen as innovative, while simultaneously emphasizing traditional values and a service-led mentality. All this has to be communicated through staff training, strategic branding and branch design, not simply though advertising – the quick fix route to shifting perceptions.

Source: Marketing 22.04.09

BUYER BEHAVIOUR AND DECISION-MAKING UNITS

Involvement theory

The split brain

Involvement theory developed from behavioural psychology research into hemispherical lateralization or split-brain theory. Very briefly, this theory is based on the following premise:

- The right and left hemispheres of the brain each specialize in the different kinds of information they process.

- The left hemisphere is responsible for cognitive activities such as reading, speaking and attribution information processing.

- The right hemisphere of the brain is concerned with nonverbal, timeless, pictorial and holistic information.

Individuals passively process and store right-brain information, whereas accepting left-brain information requires a conscious decision:

- Because it is largely pictorial, TV viewing is considered a right hemisphere activity. Passive learning is thought to occur through repeated exposures to low-involvement information. Therefore, TV advertisements are thought to produce a change in consumer behaviour *before* they change consumer attitudes.

- The left hemisphere is associated with high-involvement information. Print media (newspapers and magazines) are considered left hemisphere (or high-involvement) activity.

Right-brain theory stresses the importance of the visual component of advertising, including the creative use of symbols. Pictorial cues are more effective at generating recall and familiarity with the product, although verbal cues (which trigger left-brain processing) generate cognitive activity that encourages consumers to evaluate the advantages and disadvantages of the product.

Research suggests that the spheres of the brain do not always operate independently of each other but work together to process information. There is evidence that both sides of the brain are capable of low and high involvement. However, it does seem that the right side is more cognitively oriented and the left side more affectively oriented.

Involvement

A consumer's level of involvement in a purchase depends on the degree of personal relevance that the product holds for them:

- **High-involvement purchases** are those that are very important to the consumer in terms of perceived risk (see below).

- **Low-involvement purchases** are purchases that are not very important to the consumer, hold little relevance and little perceived risk.

- Highly involved consumers find fewer brands acceptable (they are called **narrow categorizers**).

- Uninvolved consumers are likely to be receptive to a greater number of advertising messages regarding the purchase and will consider more brands (they are **broad categorizers**).

Central and peripheral routes to persuasion

The premise here is that consumers are more likely to weigh information carefully about a product, and to devote considerable cognitive effort to evaluating it, when they are highly involved with the product category:

- Use of **the central route to persuasion** is more effective in marketing for high-involvement purchases. Thus, when involvement is high, consumers follow the central route and base their attitudes or choices on the message arguments.

- **The peripheral route to persuasion** is more effective for low-involvement purchases. When involvement is low, consumers follow the peripheral route and rely more heavily on other message elements to form attitudes or make product choices.

Marketing applications of involvement

Involvement theory has a number of strategic applications for the marketer:

- The left-brain (cognitive processing) and right-brain (passive processing) theory has strong implications for the content, length and presentation of both print and television advertisements.

- By understanding the nature of low-involvement information processing, marketers can take steps to increase consumer involvement with their ads.

- For high-involvement purchases, marketers should use arguments stressing the strong, solid, high-quality attributes of their products, thus using the central (i.e., highly cognitive) route.

QUESTION

Analyse car advertisements and assess the manufacturers use of involvement theory.

- For low-involvement purchases, marketers should use the peripheral route to persuasion, focusing on the method of presentation rather than on the content of the message (e.g. through the use of celebrity spokespersons or highly visual and symbolic advertisements).

Perceived risk

Perceived risk and involvement

The consumer's involvement grows as the level of perceived risk in the purchase of a good or service increases. It is likely that consumers will feel more involved in the purchase of their house than in the purchase of toothpaste, as the house is a much riskier purchase. Risk, in this case, is a combination of the likelihood of an unfavourable outcome and the scale of that outcome. Thus, the more likely the 'bad thing' is to happen, the higher the perceived risk, and the more damaging the 'bad thing' is felt to be, the higher the perceived risk.

Every consumer perceives some possible risks, even with purchase decisions already taken. Apprehensions about these risks are not openly expressed. Even after a transaction is completed without any risks materializing, the consumer may carry the perception that there were risks.

Types of risk

The three types of perceived risk are as follows:

1. Functional risk, of the product not performing as expected.

2. Financial risk, of having paid a higher price than necessary.

3. Risk of effort and time being wasted consequent to a possible product failure.

The direct link between perceived risk and involvement means that marketers must either

- Try to reduce the level of perceived risk in a purchase, by making messages reassuring and stressing dependability, or

- Recognize the degree of perceived risk in the purchase, and therefore the level of involvement, and tailor marketing accordingly (see the section on involvement).

Marketers can also do a lot to reassure the consumers post-purchase, on the correctness of the choice. More importantly, they should follow up every successful transaction to lay the foundation for repeat purchases and erase perception of risks.

Attitudes
What are attitudes?

An attitude describes a person's relatively consistent evaluations, feelings and tendencies towards an object or an idea.

Attitudes put people into a frame of mind for liking or disliking things and moving towards or away from them.

Companies can benefit by researching attitudes towards their products. Understanding attitudes and beliefs is the first step towards changing or reinforcing them. Attitudes are very difficult to change. A person's attitudes fit into a pattern, and changing one attitude may require making many difficult adjustments. It is easier for a company to create products that are compatible with existing attitudes than to change the attitudes towards their products.

ACTIVITY

Think about vegetarians.

There are exceptions, of course, where the high cost of trying to change attitudes may pay off.

We can now appreciate the many individual characteristics and forces influencing consumer behaviour. Consumer choice is the result of a complex interplay of cultural, social, personal and psychological factors. We, as marketers, cannot influence many of these; however, they help the marketer to better understand customers' reactions and behaviour.

DEFINITION

Attitudes can further be defined as:
  A mental predisposition to act that is expressed by evaluating a particular entity with some degree of favour or disfavour.

The tri-component model of attitude

According to the tri-component attitude model, attitude consists of three major components:

1. **The cognitive component** – This consists of a person's cognitions, that is, their knowledge and perceptions about an object. This knowledge and the resulting perceptions commonly take the form of beliefs, images and long-term memories.

2. **The affective component** – This comprises the consumer's emotions or feelings towards an object. These emotions or feelings are frequently treated, by researchers, as evaluative in nature. They capture an individual's direct or global assessment of the attitude-object, which might be positive, negative or mixed, depending on feelings about that object. The product that evokes the greatest positive (pleasurable) affective response would thus be ranked first.

3. **The conative component** – This is concerned with the likelihood or tendency of certain behaviour with regard to the attitude object. It would also mean the predisposition or tendency to act in a certain manner towards an object.

The attitude towards object model

The attitude towards object model is suitable for measuring attitudes towards a product or service category or specific brands. This model says that the consumer's attitude towards a product or specific brands of a product is a function of the presence or absence and evaluation of certain product-specific beliefs or attributes. In other words, consumers generally have favourable attitudes towards those brands that they believe have an adequate level of attributes that they evaluate as positive, and they have unfavourable attitudes towards those brands they feel do not have an adequate level of desired attributes or have too many negative or undesired attributes. For example, you may simply 'like BMWs'.

The attitude towards behaviour model

This model is the individual's attitude towards the way an object is associated with certain behaviours or characteristics. The crux of the attitude towards behaviour model is that it seems to correspond somewhat more closely to actual purchase behaviour than does the attitude towards object model. So, while you might say that you like BMWs, you might also feel that you are not ready to buy or drive one because you believe that you are too young (or maybe too old) to do so.

The theory of reasoned action model

This model represents a comprehensive integration of attitude components into a structure that is designed to lead to both better explanations and better predictions of behaviour. Similar to the basic tri-component attitude model, the theory of reasoned action model incorporates a cognitive component, an affective component and a conative component. However, these components alone are not sufficient to determine behaviour.

To understand intention, in accordance with this model, we also need to measure the subjective norms that influence an individual's intention to act. A subjective norm can be measured directly by assessing a consumer's feelings as to what relevant others would think of the action being contemplated. Would your friends laugh at you if you bought a BMW?

Attitude formation and change

We can examine attitude formation by looking at two areas:

1. How attitudes are learned. The shift from having no attitude towards a given object to having an attitude is learnt. The learning may come from information exposure, consumers' own cognition (knowledge or belief) or experience. Consumers may form an attitude before or after a purchase. Sources of influence on attitude formation include personal experience, friends and family, direct marketing or mass media.

2. Personality factors. We know that the personality of each individual is different, and it plays a very crucial role in the formation of attitude. Say for example, if you have a high need for cognition, that is, you crave for information and enjoy thinking, then you are likely to form a positive attitude in response to ads or direct mail that are rich in product-related information. On the other hand, your friend, who is relatively low in need for cognition, is more likely to form positive attitudes in response to ads that feature an attractive model or well-known celebrity.

Attitude change and persuasion

When the bank Northern Rock hit financial troubles in late 2007, customers rushed to withdraw their savings. This compounded the bank's problems. No amount of persuasive advertising by the bank and the government could stop them.

Bringing about a change in the consumer attitudes is a very important strategic consideration for marketing professionals. When the product or brand is the market leader, the marketers will work at ensuring that their customers continue to imbue their product with the existing positive attitude. Such firms also have to ensure that their existing loyal customers do not succumb to their competitor's attitude change ploys. But it is the firm whose brand is not the leader that tries to adopt marketing strategies so as to change the attitudes of the market leader's customers and win them over.

Among the attitude change strategies that are available to organizations are thefollowing:

- Changing the basic motivational function. This strategy calls for changing consumer attitudes towards a product or brand by making a new need prominent. One such method changing motivation is called the functional approach. As per this approach, attitudes can be classified in terms of four functions:

  1. **The utilitarian function** – A consumer develops a brand attitude because of its utility. In other words, we develop a favourable attitude towards a product because of how it works. So marketers try to change consumer attitudes in favour of their products or brand by highlighting its utilitarian purpose, which the competitors' consumers may not have considered.

  2. **Ego defensive function** – Most individuals want to protect their self-image. They want reassurance about their self-image from inner feelings or doubts. Firms marketing personal care and cosmetics try to appeal to this need and develop a favourable attitude change towards their products or brands by communicating a reassurance to the consumer's self-concept.

3. **The value expressive function** – A consumer develops an attitude based on general value, life style and outlook. If the target consumers hold a positive attitude towards being fashionable, then they will have a positive attitude towards high-fashion clothes.

QUESTION

How might the value expressive function work for organic food?

4. **The knowledge function** – Human nature is such that individuals prefer to know and understand the people and things they are in contact with. While product positioning, marketers try to do this and improve the consumer's attitude towards their product or brand by highlighting its benefits over competing brands.

- Associating the product with an admired group or event. At times, attitudes come to be attached to certain groups, social events or causes. So marketers could try strategies whereby their product or service comes to be associated with certain events, social groups or causes.

QUESTION

Evaluate the use of celebrity brand endorsement strategies.

- Resolving two conflicting attitudes. Marketers also try to take advantage of actual or potential conflict between attitudes. At times, firms make consumers see that their attitudes towards a brand is in conflict with another attitude, and then they may be inclined to change their evaluation of the brand.

- Altering components of the multi-attribute model. Earlier we discussed a number of multi-attribute models, which have implication for attitude change strategies. To be more precise, these models provide us with additional insights as to how to bring about attitudinal change:

1. **Changing the relative evaluation of attributes** – Consumer markets can be segmented in the same product category according to brands that offer different features or beliefs.

2. **Changing brand beliefs** – This calls for changing attitudes of consumers by changing beliefs or perceptions about the brand itself.

3. **Adding an attribute** – This means either adding an attitude that previously has been ignored or one that represents an improvement or technological innovation.

QUESTION

How has the development of mobile phones changed perceptions in relation to their functions and benefits.

4. **Changing the overall brand rating** – Altering the consumers' overall assessment of the brand directly without attempting to improve or change their evaluation of a single brand attribute. Usually this strategy employs some form of global statement like 'this is the largest selling brand'.

5. **Changing consumer beliefs about competitor's brands** – Usually it is seen that the attitude change agent is a well-respected agent authority or peer group. The amount of attitude change is related to the credibility of the source of the message. The major purpose of changing attitudes is to eventually change consumer behaviour. Thus an understanding of consumer attitudes towards their product will enable the marketer to adopt suitable strategies and create a positive image of, or attitude towards, their products in the minds of the consumer.

QUESTION

Different attitudes may exist within a B2B decision-making unit. How could you deal with this?

ACTIVITY

Pick a brand. How would you alter components of the multi-attribute model?

Cognitive dissonance theory

According to cognitive dissonance theory, discomfort or dissonance occurs when a consumer holds confusing thoughts about a belief or an attitude object (either before or after the purchase).

Post-purchase dissonance occurs after the purchase. The consumer is not happy with the purchase, so they adjust their attitudes to conform to their behaviour.

Tactics that consumers can use to reduce dissonance include reduction

- By rationalizing the decision as being wise.

- By seeking out advertisements that support the original reason for choosing the product.

- By trying to 'sell' friends on the positive features of the brand.

- By looking to known satisfied owners for reassurance.

Marketers can help reduce post-purchase uncertainty by aiming specific messages at reinforcing consumer decisions. Beyond these dissonance-reducing tactics, marketers increasingly are developing affinity or relationship programmes designed to reward good customers and to build customer loyalty and satisfaction (and, of course, repeat purchase).

Attribution theory

Attribution theory attempts to explain how people assign causality to events on the basis of either their own behaviour or the behaviour of others:

- Self-perception theory. This addresses individuals' inferences or judgements as to the cause of their own behaviour. In terms of consumer behaviour, self-perception theory suggests that attitudes develop as consumers look at and make judgements about their own behaviour. These judgements can be divided into internal, external and defensive attributions:

1. **Internal attribution** – Giving yourself credit for the outcomes – your ability, your skill or your effort.

2. **External attribution** – The purchase was good because of factors beyond your control (such as luck, or received advice).

3. **Defensive attribution** – Consumers are likely to accept credit personally for success and to attribute failure to others or to outside events.

For this reason, it is crucial that marketers offer uniformly high-quality products that allow consumers to perceive themselves as the reason for the success; that is, 'I am competent.'

- Attribution towards others. Every time you ask 'why?' about a statement or action of another – a family member, a friend, a sales person, a direct marketer a shipping company – attribution towards others theory is relevant.

- Attribution towards things. It is in the area of judging product performance that consumers are most likely to form product attributions towards things. Specifically, they want to find out why a product meets or does not meet their expectations. In this regard, they could attribute the product's successful performance (or failure) to the product itself, to themselves, to other people or situations or to some combination of these factors.

How we test our attributions

We as individuals acquire conviction about particular observations by collecting additional information in an attempt to confirm (or disconfirm) prior inferences. In collecting such information, we often use the following:

- **Distinctiveness** – The consumer attributes an action to a particular product or person if the action occurs when the product (or person) is present and does not occur in its absence.

- **Consistency over time** – Whenever the person or product is present, the consumer's inference or reaction is the same or nearly so.

- **Consistency over modality** – The inference or reaction is the same, even when the situation in which it occurs varies.

■ **Consensus** – The action is always perceived in the same way by other consumers.

GROUP INFLUENCE AND OPINION LEADERSHIP (THE CONSUMER DMU)

Reference groups

Reference groups are groups that serve as a frame of reference for individuals in their purchase decisions. This basic concept provides a valuable perspective for understanding the impact of other people on an individual's consumption beliefs, attitudes and behaviour. It also provides some insight into methods whereby groups can be used to effect desired changes in consumer behaviour.

DEFINITION

A reference group is any person or group that serves as a point of comparison (or reference) for an individual in the formation of either general or specific values, attitudes or behaviour.

The usefulness of this concept is enhanced by the fact that it places no restrictions on group size or membership nor does it require that consumers identify with a tangible group (i.e. the group can be symbolic: prosperous business people, rock stars and sports heroes).

Reference groups that influence general values or behaviour are called *normative reference groups*. An example of a child's normative reference group is the immediate family, which is likely to play an important role in moulding the child's general consumer values and behaviour (e.g. which foods to select for good nutrition, appropriate ways to dress for specific occasions, how and where to shop, what constitutes 'good' value).

Reference groups that serve as benchmarks for specific or narrowly defined attitudes or behaviour are called *comparative reference groups*. A comparative reference group might be a neighbouring family whose lifestyle appears to be admirable and worthy of imitation (the way they maintain their home, their choice of home furnishings and cars, the number and types of holidays they take).

Both normative and comparative reference groups are important. Normative reference groups influence the development of a basic code of behaviour; comparative reference groups influence the expression of specific consumer attitudes and behaviour. It is likely that the specific influences of comparative reference groups are to some measure dependent upon the basic values and behaviour patterns established early in a person's development by normative reference groups.

Types of reference group

Reference groups can be classified in terms of a person's membership or degree of involvement with the group and in terms of the positive or negative influences they have on his or her values, attitudes and behaviour. Four types of reference groups that emerge from a cross-classification of these factors:

1. A contactual group is a group in which a person holds membership or has regular face-to-face contact and of whose values, attitudes and standards he or she approves. Thus a contactual group has a positive influence (i.e. to support group's values) on an individual's attitudes or behaviour for example, membership of a netball/football team, political party.

2. An aspirational group is a group in which a person does not hold membership and does not have face-to-face contact but of which he or she wants to be a member. Thus it serves as a positive influence on that person's attitudes or behaviour for example, successful business people, atheletes, performers.

3. A disclaimant group is a group in which a person holds membership or has face-to-face contact but disapproves of the group's values, attitudes and behaviour. Thus the person tends to adopt attitudes and behaviour that are in opposition to the norms of the group (negative influence) for example, membership of a different youth tribe such as Emos or Goths.

4. An avoidance group is a group in which a person does not hold membership and does not have face-to-face contact and disapproves of the group's values, attitudes and behaviour. Thus, the person tends to adopt attitudes and behaviours that are in opposition to those of the group. For example the British National Party (BNP).

Reference group impact on choice

In some cases, and for some products, reference groups may influence both a person's product category and brand choices. Such products are called product-plus, brand-plus items. In other cases, reference groups influence only the product category decision. Such products are called product-plus, brand-minus items. In still other cases, reference groups influence the brand decision. These products are called product-minus, brand-plus items. Finally, in some cases, reference groups influence neither the product category nor the brand decision; these products are called product-minus, brand-minus items.

Reference groups and consumer conformity

Marketers are particularly interested in the ability of reference groups to change consumer attitudes and behaviour (i.e. to encourage conformity). To be capable of such influence, a reference group must

- Inform or make the individual aware of a specific product or brand.

- Provide the individual with the opportunity to compare his or her own thinking with the attitudes and behaviour of the group.

- Influence the individual to adopt attitudes and behaviours that are consistent with the norms of the group;

- Legitimize an individual's decision to use the same products as the group.

Reference group appeals have two principal benefits for the advertiser; they increase brand awareness, and they serve to reduce perceived risk:

1. **Increased brand awareness** – Reference group appeals provide the advertiser with the opportunity to gain and retain the attention of prospective consumers with greater ease and effectiveness than is possible with many other types of promotional campaigns. This is particularly true of the celebrity form of reference group appeal, where the personality employed is generally well known to the relevant target segment. Celebrities tend to draw attention to the product through their own popularity. This gives the advertiser a competitive advantage in gaining audience attention, particularly on television where there are so many brief and similar commercial announcements.

2. **Reduced perceived risk** – The use of one or more reference group appeals may also serve to lower the consumer's perceived risk in purchasing a specific product. The example set by the endorser or testimonial-giver may demonstrate to the consumer that uncertainty about the product purchase is unwarranted.

Opinion leadership

DEFINITION

Opinion leadership is . . .

The process by which one person (the opinion leader) informally influences the actions or attitudes of others, who may be opinion seekers or merely opinion recipients.

The definition of opinion leadership emphasizes informal influence. This informal flow of opinion-related influence between two or more people is often referred to as word-of-mouth communication. The biggest advantage of word-of-mouth communication is that it takes place between people who are not directly associated with the commercial selling source or the firm. Very often, we can see that word-of-mouth communication is more influential than advertising in determining which product or brand is bought.

ACTIVITY

Assess the development of social networking sites (like Facebook) which grew by opinion leadership and reference group activity; Facebook never advertised. What does this tell you about reference groups and opinion leaders.

Characteristics of opinion leaders

Let us now take a look at the main characteristics of opinion leaders. Some of the main characteristics that most opinion leaders share are the following:

- Opinion leaders are more knowledgeable and have a keen level of interest in the product or service. They are exposed to media and see more movies and television. They also read information magazines and technical publications devoted to the product category. Having greater knowledge about the product, they can disseminate more and true information about the products and their usage.

- Opinion leaders have more self-confidence, are more sociable and cosmopolitan and take more risks. They want to influence neighbours and friends, and have a wide social network.

- Opinion leaders are younger, generally have a higher education, have a higher income and higher occupational status than opinion receivers. Because of their gregarious nature, people enjoy interacting with them.

- Opinion leaders are perceived to be highly credible sources of product-related information. Opinion leaders are persons who are considered to be knowledgeable. They often voice their opinion based on first-hand information.

- Opinion leaders also have a lot of purchase experience: their experience as a shopper and user sets them apart from other people. Since most of their advice is based on first-hand experience, opinion receivers have a lot of confidence in their advice.

- Opinion leaders usually provide unbiased information, that is, they provide both favourable and unfavourable information to the opinion seekers: this adds credibility to them and opinion seekers have faith that they are receiving correct information.

Opinion leaders are therefore important to marketers, and marketing strategies are formed and evaluated keeping the opinion leaders and their roles in mind.

Opinion leadership and marketing strategy

Marketers have long been aware of the power that opinion leadership exerts on consumers' preferences and actual purchase behaviour. Many marketers look for an opportunity to encourage word-of-mouth communications and other favourable informal conversations.

New product designers take advantage of the effectiveness of word-of-mouth communication by deliberately designing products to have word-of-mouth potential. A new product should give customers something to talk about.

Proof of the power of word-of-mouth is the cases in which critics hate a movie and the viewing public like it and tell their friends. In instances where informal word-of-mouth does not spontaneously emerge from the uniqueness of the product or its marketing strategy, some marketers have deliberately attempted to stimulate or to simulate opinion leadership. The use of 'viral marketing', where opinion leaders are encouraged to pass details of a new product to friends, has become more common since the development of social networking sites such as Facebook and MySpace.

QUESTION

Evaluate the 'Bring back Wispa' campaign; is it an example of viral marketing or word-of-mouth consumer pressure?

Some product categories have professional opinion leaders who are also very influential. Hairstylists serve as opinion leaders for hair-care products. For healthcare products, pharmacists are important opinion leaders. Computer professionals can give an opinion about the purchase of personal computers. In other markets, the opinion leaders may be celebrities, such as sportspeople. The idea is to identify the opinion leaders, and then undertake a marketing research on them and formulate a marketing strategy to appeal to them.

Organizational buying behaviour

Business to business (B2B) marketing

In B2B marketing, it may be relevant for an organization to communicate not only with the purchaser but also with others who could be involved in the decision to purchase. The people involved in the purchase decision tend to have quite formal and closely defined roles; these individuals who make and influence buying decisions in a B2B environment are known as the decision-making unit (DMU).

DEFINITION

A decision-making unit (DMU) is as follows

In marketing, procurement and organizational studies, there is a group of employees, family members or members of any type of organization responsible for finalizing major decisions, usually involving a purchase. In a business setting, major purchases typically require input from various parts of the organization, including finance, accounting, purchasing, information technology management and senior management. Highly technical purchases, such as information systems or production equipment, also require the expertise of technical specialists. In some cases the DMU is an informal ad hoc group, but in other cases, it is a formally sanctioned group with specific mandates, criteria and procedures. In a generic sense, there are typically six roles within any buying centre. They are as follows:

- Initiator who suggests purchasing a product or service.
- Influencers who try to affect the outcome decision with their opinions.
- Deciders who have the final decision.
- Buyers who are responsible for the contract.
- End users of the item being purchased.
- Gatekeepers who control the information flow.

For example, a firm that supplies photocopiers to small businesses needs to communicate with a variety of people, including the adminstrative assistant who will use the machine, the office manager who has encountered other machines working in other organizations and the finance director who will be interested in how much it will cost. These are not direct customers but may influence the decision to buy and therefore need to be communicated with.

B2B purchasing behaviour

The obvious difference between industrial or institutional markets and consumer markets is that, instead of purchases being made for individual consumption, industrial markets are made for business use. There are several factors that differentiate consumer markets and their buying behaviour from organizational market and their buying behaviour.

The key factors of differentiation areas follows:

- Market structure and demand:

    1. In organizations, buyers are more geographically concentrated than consumer markets.

    2. Organizational buyers are fewer in number, but they are bulk buyers compared to individual buyers.

3. Organizational buyer markets are either vertical or horizontal. In vertical structures they cater only to one or two industries, whereas in horizontal structures the buyer base is broad.

4. Organizational demand is derived from consumer demand. The nature of the demand is fluctuating.

■ Buyer characteristics:

1. Many individuals are involved in the decision-making process.

2. Organizational buyers are quite knowledgeable and professional.

3. The buying motive is mostly more rational than that of the individual buyer.

■ Decision process and buying patterns:

1. In organizational buying, a lot of formalities like proposals, quotations and procedures are to be followed, unlike in consumer buying.

2. The decision process is much more complex, with high financial risk, technical aspects, multiple influencing factors, etc.

3. Organizational buying requires more extensive negotiation over a longer time period than consumer buying.

QUESTION

If you were a recruitment consultant, tasked with securing a major corporate client, how would you go about it?

DMU roles

Various roles within a typical DMU have been identified:

■ In the case of a substantial organization, the *initiators* might be senior management needing technology to reduce costs.

■ *Influencers* might include technical staff, such as maintenance technicians, but might also include respected advisors such as a chief executive or a senior manager from another function.

- *Deciders* might well be an individual purchasing manager or a small committee that advises on the purchase decision.

- *Approvers* might include senior financial staff, who could insist on, or veto, financial aspects of contracts such as penalty clauses for late delivery.

- The *buyers* are those who actually sign the contract or order, for example the board, and will be strongly influenced by the deciders, with little flexibility to switch vendors or change the contract.

- *Gatekeepers* would include such functions as safety (compliance of equipment with local and company safety policy, e.g. VDU use) or might be an individual such as the PA or secretary to an influencer.

- The *users* are those who will consume the product or service. Quite often they are very distant from, and exert little influence on, the decision-making process.

The reason for this DMU analysis is that not all the DMU participants will meet sales staff, so the literature and the rest of the integrated communications mix must carry the marketing message to them. The members of the DMU are key stakeholders with whom the selling organization needs to build strong links and relationships.

Considering the differing needs of the various DMU members, it can be seen that a different marketing mix may well be required for each of them.

QUESTION

You are selling cleaning products to a large manufacturing company. Who are the different players in the DMU likely to be? How would you vary the marketing mix to recognize the differing needs of each player?

Personal buying behaviour and influences

Consumer motives

Consumers have a complex mix of buying motives:

- **Product motives** – Product motives may be defined as those impulses, desires and considerations which make the buyer purchase a product. These may still be classified on the basis of nature of satisfaction:

1. Emotional product motives are those impulses that persuade the consumer on the basis of his emotion. The buyer does not try to reason out, or logically analyse, the need for purchase. The customer makes a buying decision to satisfy pride, sense of ego, urge to initiate others or a desire to be unique.

2. Rational product motives are defined as those impulses that arise on the basis of logical analysis and proper evaluation. The buyer makes a rational decision based on evaluation of the purpose, alternatives available, cost benefit and such valid reasons.

- **Patronage motives** – Patronage motives may be defined as considerations or impulses that persuade the buyer to be loyal to specific brands. Just like product motives, patronage can also be emotional or rational:

1. Emotional patronage motives are those that persuade a customer to buy specific brands, or from specific shops, without any logical reason behind this action. For example, the customer may just enjoy shopping in a 'favourite place'.

2. Rational patronage motives are those which arise when selecting a brand or shop depending on the buyer satisfaction that it offers; perhaps there is a wide selection of goods, it has the latest models or it offers good after-sales service.

Need recognition/problem solving

Recognizing that, as a consumer, your need to purchase a product or service can be for a number of reasons. It may be that you need to replace something you already own, which no longer fulfils your needs. A new father of twins may realize that his two-seater sports car is no longer the ideal car for him to own.

Other changes in your life may result in new purchases – a change of job requiring you to work from home will result in your needing office and IT facilities, or maybe you have just made a new set of friends who go skiing three times a year, so you need the equipment to join them.

Outside influences also lead to us to recognizing a need. The knowledge that the population is ageing and today's 40-year-olds will probably not receive a sufficient state pension is prompting many to top up their personal pension plans. On a different scale, did we know that we needed a disposable toilet brush before we saw one advertised on TV? Communications can be the single most powerful influence if used well.

Needs arise for different reasons, and different people will be aware of different needs, but once the need has been recognized then the consumer will be in a state of heightened attention, more likely to take notice of products/services that fulfil their needs or solve their problems.

Let us follow through an example of a couple booking for their honeymoon and see what messages and media they will be aware of as they progress through the buying process.

Information search

In this state of heightened awareness, in this case for an exotic and memorable holiday, the couple will start searching for information about their ideal honeymoon destination and itinerary.

They will search the Internet, look out for newspaper and magazine articles and advertising, walk the high street to interrogate the travel agents, listen to the radio, watch TV travel programmes and ask their friends and work colleagues about their experiences. At this stage, the message needs to be about the holiday resort. The strapline needs to conjure up the feeling of being on holiday and the visual needs to feature a long white beach, turquoise sea and palm trees.

The media will need to be carefully chosen to reach the target group – a bridal magazine will reach this couple but not other consumers for an exotic holiday.

Evaluation of alternatives

Having collated a plethora of information, the couple now need to sift through that information to make a considered decision. They will start considering their important criteria in order to sift the information – which country, which resort, hotel or self-catering, duration of flight, departing airport. At this stage, they will find information gaps and need to gain additional, more detailed information on certain options.

Websites and the travel agent can provide this information, but it needs to be easily accessible for them to retain interest in a particular holiday package. They are also looking for a USP or differentiating factor that will make their choice easier. This could be a complimentary bottle of champagne on arrival or a limo to the airport.

Whichever is likely to appeal to this couple is what the holiday company needs to be finding out and communicating to them. This message is unlikely to be the banner headline for the company, but in all the brochures, websites and travel agents it does need to be contained within the communication from the organization. The key objective here is to *inform* detail.

The purchase decision

In most cases it is the sales person either in a shop or on the phone that will move the consumer towards making a final purchase decision. In the case of online purchasing, the ease of access and navigability of the site will aid the purchase transaction, but a site that shows positive customer feedback and comprehensive resort guides will help the purchaser towards the final purchase.

It is important at this stage that there are no last-minute hitches to put off the purchaser. A crowded travel agency, ever-ringing phone or an unavailable website will mean the couple do not see the final purchase decision through and could lead to them reconsidering their decision.

Added value gained at the point of purchase can also sway a decision. A third week free could encourage people to lengthen their stay; free travel insurance can encourage them to consider another company. It is important that the messages received by the consumer at this stage help to confirm in their minds that they have made the right decision, and they feel secure in their choice. The key objective here is to *differentiate.*

QUESTION

Is booking a honeymoon a 'high involvement', 'high risk' proposition? What about compared to getting married?

Post-purchase evaluation

We cannot forget the consumer once they have made their purchase. What happens after purchase will affect their repurchasing decisions and the feedback that they give to family and friends. There need to be feedback devices incorporated within any communication so that problems can be detected early and acted upon. Front-line staff need to be competent in dealing with problems and complaints. The message here needs to be one of reassurance that problems will be sorted out and there are available resources to enable that to happen. Only if this occurs can customer satisfaction arise. The key objective here is to continue the *differentiation* to *remind* the couple why they made this choice.

DEPENDENCIES IN THE MARKETING MIX

Employee satisfaction and customer satisfaction

One way to illustrate the relation between internal operations and customer satisfaction in services is proposed in the service profit chain (SPC) by Heskett *et al.* (1994).

The SPC (Figure 3.5) has also been influenced by the analysis of successful service organizations. It is a valuable tool for managers to target new investments and to develop their service offerings and satisfaction levels for maximum competitive impact, as such widening the gap between service leaders and their merely good competitors. The SPC establishes relationships between profitability, customer loyalty, employee satisfaction, loyalty and productivity. It is not solely the various elements of the chain that are of interest, it is also the links in the chain that focus should be placed on.

The links in the chain are to be seen as sequential: each component of the SPC is influenced primarily by the previous component in the chain, as follows:

1. Customer loyalty drives profit and growth

2. Customer satisfaction drives customer loyalty

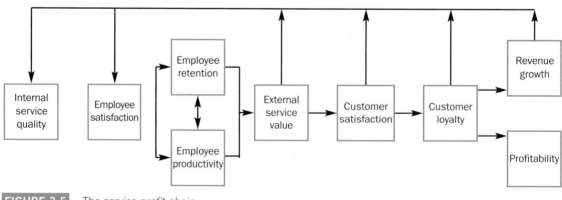

FIGURE 3.5   *The service profit chain.*
Source: *Heskett et al. (1994).*

3. Service value drives customer satisfaction

4. Employee loyalty and productivity drive service value

5. Employee satisfaction drives employee loyalty and productivity

6. Internal quality processes drive employee satisfaction.

Heskett *et al.* emphasize that the SPC is circular. A direct influence to each link stems from the previous one, but, indirectly, all links are interrelated and therefore interdependent.

The importance of customer loyalty has drawn leading service firms into trying to quantify customer satisfaction. However, today's customers are strongly value-orientated, and research programmes have shown that it is extremely important to distinguish between very satisfied and satisfied customers, as they have different repurchasing behaviour. Customers perceive value as the results they receive in relation to the total costs. Therefore, many organizations have started to measure relationships between individual links in the SPC.

The first links of the SPC, which can be viewed as the starting point, constitute the internal service delivery systems. This encompasses, according to Heskett *et al.*, internal service quality, employee satisfaction, employee retention and employee productivity. The main focus is solely on employee satisfaction, which, in return, has a direct influence on employee retention and productivity. According to the model, the latter has a positive influence on the value of services provided to external customers.

QUESTION

Many organizations now routinely monitor, and proactively manage, staff 'engagement' with the organization. How might this be done?

Reichheld

The main focus of the Service Profit Chain is the relation between internal operations, customer satisfaction and loyalty. The importance of customer loyalty is stressed by Reicheld and Sasser (1990). They suggest that companies should be aware of the disadvantages concerning defection of customers, as well as the positive aspects of loyal customers. They estimate that a

5 per cent increase in customer loyalty could produce profit increases from 25 per cent to 85 per cent.

Reichheld re-draws the SPC as a circle and calls it the 'service profit cycle' (see Figure 3.6). This reinforces the fact, mentioned by the original authors, that each element of the chain is related to each of the others.

Customer and stakeholder management

The proactive management of customers is at the core of customer relationship management (CRM), which has been discussed earlier. Revenue comes from customers. Good customer management is essential, and it is now being recognized that there is a very strong link between customer management performance and overall business performance. Doing this means understanding which customers are profitable and which are not and then acquiring, retaining and developing the right customers in the most efficient way.

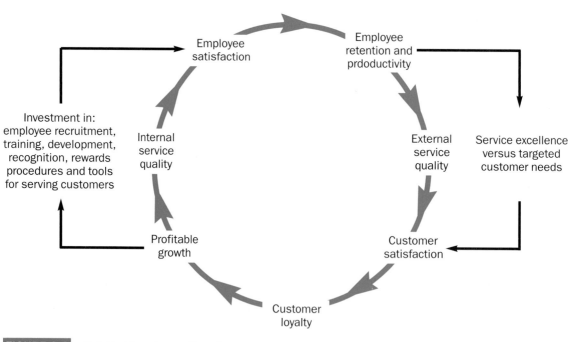

FIGURE 3.6 *Reichheld service profit cycle.*

Customer management involves a comprehensive understanding of customer needs as either individual customers or segments of customers. Propositions need to be developed that will match the needs of these customers and will be attractive to new customers.

Customer Management Activity (CMA) is about implementing the plans to deliver the proposition across the Customer Life Cycle from initial targeting, handling enquiries through to winning back lost customers. Customers may have a good or bad experience at each life cycle stage and make comparisons between their suppliers.

Everyone in the organization should be customer focused when interacting with both external and internal customers. Having the right people, processes, customer information and technology help enable good customer management. Leaving customer management to functional departments results in silo customer management, implying inefficiencies and a dysfunctional (and unfulfilling) customer experience.

Stakeholder relationship management takes the concept of proactive customer management and extends it to apply to all the organization's stakeholders. It combines the principles of stakeholder marketing with those of supply chain management.

Product development

Earlier in this unit, we looked at the development of products in response to customer needs, but how do we actually do that?

The idea of actually getting stakeholders involved in the new product development process originates both in stakeholder marketing and in supply chain management. For some time, organizations have involved, for example, a supplier in process redesign or a customer in product development. Taking a 'partnering' approach to the development of products can have significant benefits to the organization, including the following:

- Faster development and a shorter time to market, as many people can be working on a product development in parallel.

- Reduced R&D costs, as costs are shared with partners.

- Better solutions, that more closely fit with stakeholder needs.

- Improved creativity, due to the 'brainstorming' aspects of collaborative development.

INSIGHT

Collaborative knowledge building on the Internet is as old as the Internet itself. For a long time, free sharing of information has been a central aspect of Internet culture ('information wants to be free' used to be a popular slogan). Simple collaborative environments such as e-mail lists have existed since the early 1970s, and slightly more advanced systems such as Usenet and Bulletin Board Systems (BBSs) since the early 1980s. However, with the commercialization of the Internet in 1990s, and the success of the Free and Open Source Software, it has been recognized that collaborative development of knowledge is a particular and innovative practice that requires a distinct social, technical and legal framework to succeed. Socially, it requires an understanding by the participants of the merits of collaboration and a willingness not only to just share one's own knowledge but also to accept that other people might transform that knowledge in unexpected ways.

Instead of a clear separation between author and audience, expert and novice, we have a situation in which everyone is entitled to read and write. Technically, specialized platforms support this process by making it easy for people to build on other people's contributions and by ensuring transparency how a resource has been transformed. Legally the traditional conception of copyright, which gives the author nearly unlimited control over the use of his/her works, is being replaced by copyleft which is based on the nearly unlimited rights to distribute and adapt works.

Perhaps the most prominent example of Open Source Intelligence project is the free online encyclopaedia, Wikipedia. Technically, it is based on a Wiki platform, which allows everyone with a standard web browser to edit page. The software keeps a history of the modifications of a page, making it easy to see how the content developed over time and, if necessary, remove unqualified modifications or vandalism.

Founded in early 2001, it has grown to over 450,000 articles by the end of 2004, all written by volunteers without central editing or coordination. It is published under the GNU Free Documentation licence. Many of these articles can match the level of quality found in commercial encyclopaedias, while others are still below standard. As a recent IBM study showed, the project – despite its openness – is surprisingly stable and resistant to misuse. Its history so far gives reason for optimism that articles will improve over time, as knowledgeable people will fill in the gaps that still exist and collaborative editing will remove errors that are still present.

Eric S. Raymond, a leading analyst of the Free and Open Source Software movement, once expressed the underlying assumption in the following way: 'Given enough eyeballs, all bugs are shallow.' He meant that people with different skills and knowledge domains will find different errors easy to spot and correct. What is a hard problem for one person might be trivial for someone else. If there are enough people who look at page, all errors will be found and removed. Like all collaborative projects, Wikipedia is a living project that changes constantly, rather than being a fixed product to which updates are made available to the public from time to time.

Other prominent examples include the Indymedia network of community-based alternative news, the collaborative editing site kuro5hin, and, to a lesser degree, user-built databases such as the CDDB, which contains information on sound files.

Source: Vecam.com

QUESTION

How could your organization use stakeholder collaboration in the development of new products or services? Which stakeholders would you invite to participate?

INSIGHT

The development programme called Open Innovation Challenge is a pilot collaboration between the National Endowment For Science, Technology and the Arts (Nesta), British Design Innovation, Oakland Innovation and P&G. If it is successful, more large companies will pledge their interest.

Participants will be invited to submit proposals for products which fit P&G's criteria and have the potential to build businesses worth over $100 million (£50 million). To protect their intellectual property, the ideas will not be seen by P&G but will be reviewed by Nesta, BDI and Oakland Innovation.

Ten of the most promising proposals will be selected and entrants given access to feedback, advice and up to £25,000 so that their ideas can be developed to a stage where they demonstrate commercial viability.

Up to five of the strongest applicants will then have the chance to present their finalized ideas to P&G. The FMCG giant will have 90 days in which to decide whether to invest in the idea and sign appropriate contracts, otherwise the creator will be free to take their proposition to other brands or investors. As is customary in such cases, the innovator will retain its IP in either instance.

Is this the shape of things to be expected, when companies plan product development in the future?

Source: iMedia

INSIGHT

Tapscott and Williams created the term 'prosumer' to describe the relationship that Lego® enjoy with their customers. This was one of the earliest, and still most vibrant, examples of a collaborative community based around a product and its development.

When Lego started to focus on high-tech toys, as opposed to the interlocking plastic bricks, they developed Logo Mindstorms, which allow purchasers to build real robots. Within a few weeks of the product launch user groups had formed and enthusiasts had reverse engineered nearly all of the components at the heart of the robotic system.

Lego's initial reaction was to threaten prosecution but, when users rebelled, the company decided to incorporate the users' ideas, even writing a 'right to hack' into the Mindstorms software licence, giving hobbyists free rein in how they might modify their purchased product. Lego uses mindstorms.lego.com to actively encourage tinkering with its product and the website offers a free, downloadable software development kit. In return Lego's customers use the site to post descriptions of their creations and detail software modifications, programming instructions and component designs that are required.

The company benefits enormously from the work of this volunteer business web. Each time a customer posts to the site the product becomes more valuable. Senior vice president Mads Nipper commented, 'Although users don't get paid for it, they enhance the experience you can have with the basic Mindstorm set – it's a great way to make the product more exciting.'

Place

According to Kotler and Lee (2007), organizations are increasingly finding that they need multiple forms of distribution channel, to take into account the differing needs of customers. Such channels as e-commerce, direct selling, mail order and retail must all work in parallel, as the emphasis in marketing shifts from the product to the service augmentation surrounding it. Alongside these multiple distribution channels, promotion must also be used to inform, educate and persuade stakeholders.

Increasingly, the relationship between an organization and its stakeholders (government, community, employees, suppliers, etc.) is becoming more reliant on emerging, primarily digital, technologies. The use of the Internet, and its 'spin-off' variants (intranet, extranet) are now, for many organizations, the primary communication channel as opposed to a 'niche' add-on.

The major implications of the Internet for the place aspect of the marketing mix are covered by the following sections.

Place of purchase

McDonald and Wilson (2002) identified five options:

- **Seller-controlled sites** – main sites of supplier companies, which are e-commerce enabled (Norwich Union, in the insurance market).

- **Seller-oriented sites** – controlled by third parties but represent the seller rather than providing a full range of options (The AA or RAC).

- **Neutral site** – independent evaluator intermediaries that enable price and product comparison and will result in the purchase being fulfilled on the target site (GoCompare).

- **Buyer-oriented sites** – controlled by third parties on behalf of the buyer (MoneyExpert).

- **Buyer-controlled sites** – involve either procurement posting on buyer-company sites or those of intermediaries that have been set up in such a way that it is the buyer who initiates the market making.

QUESTION

These intermediaries become stakeholders, but the organization may not even know about their existence. How might you research this phenomenon, and its impact on your organization?

Navigation

Four key aspects were proposed by Evans and Wurster (1999):

- **Reach** – The potential audience of the e-commerce site. Reach can be increased by moving from a single site to representation with a large number of different intermediaries.

- **Richness** – The depth or detail of information that is both collected about the customer and provided to the customer. This is related to the product element of the mix.

- **Affiliation** – Refers to whose interest the selling organization represents – consumers or suppliers. This particularly applies to retailers, suggesting that customers will favour retailers who provide them the richest information on comparing products.

- **Localization** – The strategy of providing a local site, most of the times using the local language. Local sites are especially important when the culture differences are significant from one marketplace to another, and the organization finds it more appropriate to address locally.

ACTIVITY

Search the Internet for different ways to buy any commonly purchased product. Look at the options identified by McDonald and Wilson and the issues raised by Evans and Wurster. Are they still valid? (2002 and 1999 are 'a very long time ago' in Internet terms!)

MEASURING THE SUCCESS OF THE MARKETING MIX

In considering which media to use within a communications campaign, one of the factors that influences our choice is 'what has worked well in the past', so it is important that we can effectively evaluate what each medium has contributed towards the overall campaign results.

Accountants and marketers have long argued about the measurability and accountability of spending what is probably the single biggest expenditure that the organization makes.

Television is perhaps the most audited of the above-the-line tools. Day-by-day, minute-by-minute audience figures tell us who is watching at any time during the 24-hour day. Digital television has introduced two-way communication, so for the first time we can actually measure the audience's response by the number of 'red buttons' clicked. The inclusion of website addresses and direct response telephone numbers has also introduced a measurable aspect into television advertising.

But, in real terms, the role of advertising is to develop long-term brand values, and the benefit of the expenditure can only be measured by a shift in customer attitudes over time. This is also true of all other above-the-line media in that although they all have a short-term measurable aspect to their use, their real value is as a strategic tool used consistently over time. It is not coincidence that some of the world's icon brands such as Coca-Cola, IBM and Kellogg's are also those that have consistently appeared in the top-ten-advertising spend tables over the last 10 years.

Is it the role of marketing research to measure these shifts over time on both a brand/service level and within the marketplace? It is really the only way we get a complete picture of how customers perceive our offering.

There will always be significant debate about the validity and effectiveness of the advertising pound. We now have to communicate to compete and we are now in possession of more information than ever before. We now have to learn how that information can be used effectively.

Inquiry tests

To measure the response to a sales promotion campaign that used a '20p off' coupon you could set up a system with retailers to count the number of redeemed vouchers. By media coding the coupon, you will know which magazine produced the most responses.

Similarly, the response rates from direct marketing campaigns should be evaluated and, if appropriate, a further check made to calculate how much response is actually converted to sales. This way the cost of a campaign can be measured against the monetary gain from sales.

Recall tests

Tests of how much the viewer of an advertisement remembers of the message; they are used to measure the cognitive residue of the ad. These are the most commonly employed tests in advertising

Recognition tests

Tests in which audience members are asked whether they recognize an advertisement or something in an advertisement. These are the standard cognitive residue test for print ads and promotion.

Sales

It is not appropriate to only look at sales when you are measuring the success of an advertisement or a campaign, because other factors in the marketing mix or the external environment could affect sales (in either a negative or a positive way). For example, if there was media coverage of a research report suggesting that chocolate improved your IQ and reduced stress at the same time as the 'Chocco' advertising campaign, then this could be the reason for a sales increase and not the effect of the advertising campaign. Or, perhaps weather conditions could affect cocoa production adversely, which could cause price rises and reduce demand for 'Chocco', no matter how effective the advertising campaign.

Tracking studies

Studies that document the apparent effect of advertising over time. Commonly, tracking studies assess attitude change, knowledge, behavioural intent and self-reported behaviour. They are one of the most commonly used advertising and promotion research methods.

Financial analysis

Financial analysis attempts to track the impact of marketing on sales, profit and share price. The main problem with such detailed analysis is isolating the cause of any change. It is almost impossible to separate the impact of marketing from that of other variables such as the economy, competitor activity and seasonality.

Media evaluation

Within the promotional message, the evaluation has two elements to consider, the content of the message itself and how well that worked at communicating and the efficiency of the media chosen in transmitting the message.

The message content can be evaluated either by commissioning marketing research or by looking at the accuracy in the feedback we are getting from the consumer. If they are entering retail stores asking for the product or lots of people are walking round singing our jingle, we can assume the message is getting through.

The effectiveness of the media can also be measured by marketing research, but although we may be conscious that awareness has risen to 80 per cent, how can we judge which media helped to achieve that the most?

Stakeholder satisfaction surveys

Good service is the lifeblood of any business. Although new customers are important, good service will help generate customer loyalty and repeat business. With each satisfied customer a business is likely to win many more customers through recommendations. Remember, if you are not taking care of your customers, your competition will.

A stakeholder satisfaction survey will help an organization not only to see how effective its efforts have been, but also to identify problem areas for further action. It will also demonstrate to stakeholders that the organization cares and is proactively looking for ways to improve the service that it provides.

QUESTION

Supplier questionnaires – 'How good are we as customers?' Staff satisfaction surveys – 'Are we a caring employer?' Are these appropriate questions?

As well as obtaining valuable market research data, stakeholder surveys are also a good way to publicize aspects of an organization's service that its stakeholders may not be aware of. It is important to read through a survey from a market research view point to check that it asks the right questions in the right way and that with the feedback information it will be possible to make informed decisions. Then, read through the survey from a marketing viewpoint, checking that each question is phrased in such a way that every opportunity has been taken to promote the business.

To benefit most from a survey, the organization needs to be prepared to accept the worst. A survey should be designed to highlight problems so that they can be addressed; satisfaction will prevent complacency and will also give early warning on where competitors' initiatives may be losing the organization business.

INSIGHT

Arthur C. Nielsen Sr. founded his namesake company in 1923 to perform surveys of the production of industrial equipment. Over time, however, he saw a larger opportunity in helping companies take the mystery out of their marketing. As the retail pioneer John Wanamaker once famously mused: 'I know I waste half my money on advertising. I just don't know which half.' Nielsen set out to solve that riddle by counting, measuring and analysing what people buy, eat, read, watch, listen to and otherwise consume. In the process, he fathered one of the most powerful business concepts of the twentieth century: market share. Today, as it happens, Nielsen is headquartered in the refurbished Wanamaker's department store building in Manhattan.

Having popularized the idea of market share, Nielsen Sr. and son Arthur Nielsen Jr. made sure over the years to seize as much of it as possible. Nowhere were they more successful than with the television ratings system, launched in 1950, that made Nielsen a household name. Almost six decades later the service still functions as a near-monopoly. Nielsen has honed its methods over the years, but some ad buyers and media executives are still critical that Nielsen derives its national TV ratings from a mere 14,000 'Nielsen families' who have meters hooked up to their TVs. Nielsen also rates local and cable viewership, among other things. Altogether, Nielsen Media Research makes up roughly one-third of the company's $4.5 billion in sales.

Another third of the company's revenues is generated by A.C. Nielsen, which commands more than 60 per cent of the retail research market globally. Overall, the company gathers data by employing two separate armies. One comprises some 31,000 people worldwide who do nothing but organize and retrieve retail sales figures from stores. The other includes more than 700,000 people who participate in ongoing research panels in which, for modest sums, they anonymously lay their consumption patterns bare to Nielsen's statisticians.

How do companies use Nielsen's data? Say Nestlé wants to introduce a new flavour of Häagen-Dazs ice cream. For starters, Nielsen can tell them that Pittsburgh is the icecream buying capital of America. (Who knew?) One Nielsen business, BASES, can forecast how the flavour will do before a single pint is produced. Another can determine the best addresses to locate a new Häagen-Dazs shop. The main A.C. Nielsen figures can parse by market how the flavour is doing against rivals. And the media side of Nielsen can help figure out how and where ads are sold and even monitor passing mentions of it on TV shows and blogs.

Source: Siklos, R. (2008) Made to Measure [online] in 'Fortune' at http://money.cnn.com/2008/02/18/news/news-makers/siklos_calhoun.fortune/index2.htm accessed 28 February 08.

ACTIVITIES

Practice work-based project

Using the marketing mix

Kotler and Lane Keller (2006) define the marketing mix as the set of controllable variables and their levels that the firm uses to influence the target market.

The manager must address these fundamental areas so that all 'the Ps' combine to emphasize marketing as a total system of coordinated organizational activity focused on satisfying customer needs. There are clearly a wide variety of possible combinations of marketing variables which management can select. Inevitably some combinations will earn greater financial returns than others.

Role

You have been asked to present a proposal to the Marketing Manager that contains a set of recommendations to utilize the marketing mix to support stakeholder relationships. These recommendations should focus on the use of the marketing mix in relation to a 'breakthrough' product/service that your organization is planning to launch in the near future. (Note: In order to protect the intellectual property of your organization, this proposed product/service should be hypothetical – that is, invented by you for the purpose of this assessment.)

Produce a formal report for your Marketing Manager in which you

- Provide a brief background to your chosen organization, its products/services, customer base, position in market (two sides of A4 maximum, to be included as an appendix).

- Provide a brief background to the new product/service your organization is planning to launch, the target customer segment(s) for that product/service, potential competitors and any other issues you feel to be significant to the launch.

- Explain how the concepts of 'involvement' and 'attitudes' might be relevant to the 'decision making unit' for any one target customer for the new product/service.

- Identify two internal stakeholders and two external stakeholders (excluding customer or consumer) that might be relevant to the proposed product/service launch.

- For each of the four stakeholders identified above, provide detailed recommendations for a suitable marketing mix (recognizing and including each of the seven Ps).

- Identify and evaluate a range of methods that you could utilize to measure the success of the marketing mix for any one of the stakeholders identified.

Notes on practice work-based project

Guidance on tackling the assignment

This assignment is an opportunity to use marketing mix tools in relation to the impact on internal and external stakeholder groups of a new break-through product. Having first applied their knowledge of concepts relating to the DMU, candidates are to recommend a marketing mix for each stakeholder group chosen.

Formal report

Relationship marketing concepts and theories should be appropriately applied to reflect understanding. The marketing mixes should relate to operational marketing activity, and it is not expected that candidates suggest strategic options. Moreover, candidates should be creative in their suggestions and how they communicate these.

The report should include marketing mixes to develop long-term win-win relationships with internal and external stakeholder groups. Candidates should identify how to evaluate the success of one of their marketing plans, and qualitative and quantitative methods should be considered. Candidates need to demonstrate the application of these measures in the context of the assignment. It is not sufficient to produce a generic series of measures, which may not be appropriate to the context.

In producing the report, it is important that the candidate adopts a structure and style that naturally lend themselves to reporting on the outcome of their study. The format and approach used will be driven by the relevant themes and emerging issues arising from the research. A formulaic task-based approach should be avoided. The examiners will be looking for a more holistic approach where there is clear evidence of insightful analysis, originality and clarity of expression. The report should be in a professional style with references to conceptual marketing theory included as appropriate.

Further work

- Identify how the marketing mix is used in any business-to-business transaction with which you are familiar. Consider each role in the DMU.

- For any service of which you are a consumer, identify and discuss each stage in the Service Profit Chain.

- Identify a range of stakeholders that you feel your organization should regard as 'key players'. For each stakeholder, outline how you might measure the extent to which that stakeholder is satisfied with your organization's performance.

Communicating with Stakeholders

Syllabus Content

4.1 Evaluate the extensive range of marketing communications mix tools and explain how they can be co-coordinated to contribute towards developing long-term sustainable stakeholder relationships.

4.2 Identify and evaluate the range of tools available to support the communications relating to internal customer loyalty, that is, employee support, engagement, and retention within the organization.

4.3 Explain the challenges in communicating with stakeholders in international markets.

4.4 Identify and evaluate the continuously evolving impact of new technologies and their contribution to economic and environmental sustainability on stakeholder relationships.

4.5 Explain approaches to managing budget resource for tactical communication activities.

4.6 Explain the methods available for measuring the success of coordinated marketing communications activities.

THE COMMUNICATIONS MIX

DEFINITION

The communications mix can be defined as

The particular combination of marketing tools that work together to communicate the marketer's message, to achieve the marketer's objectives, and to satisfy the target market.

Source: Allbusiness.com

In this section, we examine the elements of the communications mix and evaluate their effectiveness in promoting stakeholder relationships.

Advertising

When combining the promotional tools together to produce a customized communications package that meets the needs of our own organization, it is important to consider how each of the tools we use will complement and support each other in achieving the organization's promotional objectives. Some methods more naturally slot into the role of *primary* media, enabling mass communication and building awareness on a large scale. These tend to be above-the-line media. The promotional toolbox contains the following *above-the-line* media:

- Television
- Press
- Radio
- Outdoor
- Cinema
- Point of sale
- Internet
- Branding.

Much of the inter-media decisions taken will depend not only on the budget available but also on the media characteristics that the brand/

service requires in order that it be communicated in the best possible way. In looking at each of the media we must also consider their ability to communicate:

■ At a visual level

■ At an audio level and

■ At the right level of detail.

While advertising is commonly used, it is relatively ineffective in the context of stakeholder relationship management. Advertising tends to be an impersonal tool, whereas relationships are individual. While advertising has the potential to reach very large target markets, relationship management concentrates on one-to-one communication.

Shareholders tend to favour advertising as a communications method, as they perceive the impact of advertising to be, perhaps, greater than it actually is. Shareholders aspire to being associated with a 'big' brand and will therefore appreciate any media that raise the brand's profile, whether this translates into sales or not.

Within the decision-making unit (DMU) for any product or service, whether it be B2C or B2B, there will be a variety of attitudes and different degrees of involvement. Advertising is, by its nature, a 'blanket' method, so it is unlikely that any advertisement, unless very general, could meet the expectations of every member of the DMU.

Advertising not only (assuming it is targeted effectively) reaches the target audience, it also comes to the attention of a wide 'accidental' or 'unintended' audience. While these parties may not be directly interested in the content of the advertisement, they may be offended by it. This may lead to conflict between the organization and a key stakeholder – the 'community' in which its products are marketed. There will also be pressure groups (see Unit 1) representing moral, religious or other viewpoints, viewing the advertisement to see whether they should object to it.

In most countries, advertising is one of the most tightly controlled forms of communication. In the UK, for example, the Advertising Standards Authority (ASA) will be interested in the content of any advertisement. The ASA aims to ensure that any advertisement 'should not mislead, cause harm, or offend'.

INSIGHT

Children are being increasingly exposed to sexual imagery and their parents have limited opportunities to stop it, a report for the Home Office warns. The report calls for tougher regulation of sexual imagery in adverts and a ban on selling 'lads' mags' to under-16s.

It also recommends selling mobile phones and games consoles with parental controls automatically switched on. Author Dr Linda Papadopoulos said there was a clear link between sexualized imagery and violence towards females. Her report said the material children were being exposed to included the growth of lads' mags and pornography on mobile phones, through to big-name fashion brands using sexual imagery to advertise clothes targeted at young teenagers. She also recommends giving the ASA the power to act against sexualized imagery appearing within commercial websites, such as provocative photo-shoots used by clothing chains targeting teenagers. The review forms part of the Home Office's broader attempts to have a louder public debate about how to combat violence against women and girls.

Source: BBC News 26.02.10

A final stakeholder group that is likely to scrutinize any advertising in minute detail is the organization's competitors. They will be interested in seeing how similar or different advertising messages are from their own and in identifying any 'comparative comment' that might reflect badly on their brand. While comparative advertising is legal in the UK, any advertiser must have evidence to support any claims made. Comparisons that mention specific competitors or their products must therefore be factual, rather than subjective.

RNID

The RNID launched an interactive outdoor campaign that used moving posters that reacted to sounds around them. Set on outdoor TV screens with microphones embedded in them, the posters' messages were coded to appear as different visualizations of sound, such as a soundwave or a graphic equalizer. Created by M&C Saatchi, the campaign is based on research that indicated one in seven people are hearing impaired. The campaign used a set of negative straplines that dramatized the parts of life that people with hearing problems would still prefer to hear than not. Lines of copy could be amended to suit the area in which the poster site was positioned such as outside a concert hall.

Source: Campaign 21.08.09

ACTIVITY

Produce a stakeholder map for a national TV advertising campaign, identifying the power and interest of the various stakeholder groups.

Public relations

> ### DEFINITION
>
> The Institute of Public Relations has defined public relations as
>> *The planned and sustained effort to establish and maintain goodwill and mutual understanding between an organization and its publics.*

Public relations is essentially concerned with developing a corporate personality that communicates the general philosophies of that organization to its public. The PR activities therefore fall into four main categories:

1. Development of the corporate image – the face of the company.

2. Communication of that image and all that falls within it.

3. Specific related activities where the image is used.

4. Protection of the corporate image from adverse publicity.

The spectrum of public relations is increasing all the time in an era where there is little discernible difference between products and services. It is often the customer's perception of the *corporate personality* that PR seeks to create that offers the differentiation point.

Public relations can convey greater *credibility* than an advertising message, as it is perceived to have originated from a more independent source. The credibility of the newspaper that is reporting on the organization will be considered rather than the organization itself.

Cost is relatively low in comparison to advertising. The cost of a press conference is relatively of good value when you consider the amount of press reporting and TV coverage you can achieve with a good PR message.

Communication to the correct target audience is reliant on the PR department (or PR agency) ensuring that all the relevant press attend the conference or that the vehicle to be sponsored is one that has links to the target audience.

Control can be an issue. Although you can make sure the press have all the information to pass on a positive perception to the stakeholders, if a particular journalist is looking for a more sensational story that day, then he/she can re-position the information to give a negative slant.

Public relations covers the following activities:

- Corporate image and corporate social responsibility

- Exhibitions, conferences and special events

- Press conferences

- Press releases

- Sponsorship.

Public relations often suffers the same drawbacks in relationship management as advertising – much PR activity is aimed at a broad market, rather than individual stakeholders. There are therefore risks that any messages intended for one stakeholder might also be received by others.

QUESTION

How could you 'target' PR activities at individual stakeholders? Would this diminish the effectiveness of such activities? Would it increase the overall cost of PR?

Of all the elements of the communications mix, PR is the one that is most likely to bring the organization into contact with a wide range of stakeholders. This is because of the diversity of PR activity. PR can be specifically directed towards a range of stakeholders:

- Government (or governmental agencies) can be lobbied for support or in an attempt to change policy or legislation.

- Shareholders and the investment community (bankers and advisors) can be briefed on organizational performance or annual results.

- Journalists can be given press releases or an exclusive insight into the views or workings of the organization.

- Pressure groups can be briefed on issues that are relevant to each of them, for example, the organization's environmental or ethical policies and performance.

ACTIVITY

Find examples of recent PR activity for each of the above.

Npower and the Barmy Army

Npower is one of the English Cricket Board's (ECB) most important and long-term partners. It decided to maximize the effect of its official sponsorship by tying up with unofficial England supporters club, the Barmy Army. In 2009, alongside the official sponsorship programme, which included the Ashes, Npower teamed up with the Barmy Army to host the Npower Fans' Ashes. A team selected from the ranks of the Barmy Army took on the Fanatics (its Australian equivalent) in a series of Twenty20 matches with two celebrity players joining each side.

Source: Marketing 21.10.09

New media

Technological developments in communications are making massive changes to your personal and working lives. They are changing the way you shop, find out information, communicate with others inside and outside your organization; they are affecting the way organizations promote their products/services and even changing the way organizations do business with suppliers and distributors. Digital outdoor is becoming an increasingly common site for commuters, as moving images capture their attention on sites across the country. The technology has evolved even further, with the ability to stream live advertising messages on the screens.

Launch of the Nokia N97 handset

CBS Outdoor used streaming technology for Nokia's campaign to launch its N97 handset, using the message 'online as it happens'. Live streams were fed to digital escalator panels and cross track projections displayed Londoners' Facebook status updates, news feeds from Reuters and applications from Nokia's online platform Ovi.

Electronic point of sale (EPOS) systems allow retailers to record and monitor sales data. Linked to 'smart' card purchases, EPOS data provide organizations with detailed profiles of customer preferences and purchasing habits. Databases can be used to store information about customer purchase history so that mail-merged documents can be sent to customers with offers tailored to their needs.

INSIGHT

T-Mobile's 'flashmobbing' advertisement 'Life's for sharing' where commuters break into a dance routine at London's Liverpool Street train station is in the top 100 viewed YouTube clips. The advertisement gained such a following that the railway station was forced to close after 13,000 people turned up there for a silent disco. Its success proves that brands need to give consumers control if they want to thrive in the viral and online arena.

One criticism often leveled at virals is that they make consumers smile, but they cannot convey complex marketing messages. With the price comparison site Comparethemarket.com, VCCP had a clear brief – the brand name, which was similar to those of its rivals in a crowded market, needed to achieve awareness and recall with consumers. Enter Alexsandr the Meerkat, complete with his own website, Facebook page, viral video bloggers and, uniquely, a branded Twitter feed. George Everett, the planner at VCCP behind the campaign, the viral element made the TV campaign more effective. 'Facebook and Twitter are fantastic media for us as they allow us to build a conversation with consumers'.

Source: Marketing 29.04.10

ACTIVITY

Consider the use of customer loyalty cards, such as those common in supermarkets. How does this impact on segmentation, customer profiling and marketing activities?

Even the way you use the telephone has changed. Mobile telephones mean you can be constantly in touch with colleagues and customers even when you are away from the office. People can leave voice mail and fax messages at any time, without having to rely on others to take the information down correctly. Text messages are even considered an appropriate way to communicate with colleagues. Businesses can deal speedily with massive telephone response through voice mail and automated processes.

We are now seeing the general use of videophone technology combined with mobile phones, which will change the way you communicate on the telephone, because your body language and facial expressions can be observed. This is also a good way to reduce travel costs and 'carbon footprint'.

Laptop computers mean that you can work away from your desk or while on the move and still access or send information to your colleagues at the office. Wireless technology has removed the need for a docking station or physical connection to access the Internet, while 3G cards and Blackberries have enabled constant connection to e-mail accounts.

The advent of electronic communication has probably had the most impact, and e-mail in particular has become so popular that for many people it is the main way they communicate with others. However, it is also true to say that new ways of working still have to develop acceptable ways of working and a sense of business etiquette guiding their use.

The ability to use the Internet has had a massive impact on the speed and cost of communicating, especially accessing information on websites or transacting business online.

You can also produce vast quantities of text, sound and picture information and store it on CD-ROM or in digital versatile disc (DVD) format, which is an extremely interactive way for customers to access information. ISDN, and more recently broadband, lines have led to complex downloadable information being transmitted quickly and without the need for the now almost-redundant motorcycle courier.

INSIGHT

The development of broadband technology demonstrates the impact that the digital evolution can have in terms of channel structure and the strategic shift that organizations need to make in order to remain competitive.

Films are traditionally marketed first through cinemas, then through video releases and finally through television (as video on demand, then pay-for channels and then terrestrial services). The full financial potential is realized through this channel structure. The development of digital technologies and Internet facilities offer certain advantages to film studios, but it is not necessarily to their advantage to cut out these intermediaries. For example, not all films are successful, and it is sometimes necessary to go 'straight to video' in which case the video rental store plays a significant part in the marketing channel.

Broadband services enable people to see films online, whenever and wherever they want. For organizations such as Blockbuster video rental stores, this development has posed a major threat. With 65 million cardholders and 6300 stores worldwide (Oliver, 2000), the company needed to anticipate the changes in supply and demand. Blockbuster's response was to change the fundamental purpose or mission of the organization to be an overall entertainment provider for the home. The development of e-commerce facilities has been a key part of their strategy.

Central to this strategy was the nonexclusive digital download and video streaming rights agreement with the film studio MGM and independent film operator Atom-Films. This enables Blockbuster to showcase selected films on its website (www.block-buster.com). (This first step may lead to agreements with other studios and may well prove attractive to other entertainment-based companies that might enter into partnership deals.)

The website also enables people to purchase CDs, DVDs and games, as well as the core product, videos. In addition, Blockbuster has used interactive technologies to provide a higher level of customer personalization in the services they offer. For example, its 'Blockbuster Recommends' facility suggests films to customers based upon their previous selections or a list of films rated *I hate it or*

I like it. Another example of the personalization approach is the facility to suggest films to match the mood of the viewer. For example, if someone is feeling depressed then it may suggest a Gene Wilder film to cheer them up. All of these changes have been supported with a substantial off-line advertising campaign to inform current customers of the changes and to remind them of the Blockbuster proposition and values, to attract and persuade potential new customers to visit the site or a local store and finally to reposition the brand by differentiating it from its previous position and its main competitors.

Effectively, the company has revised its strategy to accommodate changes in the environment, implemented the necessary changes to its offering, and then re-branded itself to be repositioned in the home entertainment business.

Source: Fill (2002)

QUESTION

Blockbuster now has to compete with new business models, such as that adopted by Lovefilm – offering unlimited DVD rentals, by post, for a fixed monthly fee. How might they respond?

ACTIVITY

Critically review your organization's website and identify any opportunities to increase its effectiveness in stakeholder communications.

Internet access is now available in over 50 per cent of homes in the UK. Although the profile of users is becoming closer to the national profile, it is still heavily utilized by younger and more affluent people. Over 50 per cent of the e-mail usage emanates from people under 25 years of age.

Internet advertising allows varying levels of visual, audio and interactive messages to be developed dependent upon the budget and creativity of the designer. A great deal of information can be transmitted, with the level of interaction being determined by the 'viewer'. Usage will fall into two broad categories: the viewer who requires a specific piece of information to act upon or those who are 'browsing' – any advertising needs to fulfil the needs of both.

QUESTION

Identify examples of interactive communications that require or encourage a response (for example, polls or feedback requests). How might these be used in your organization?

All *off line* communications must feature the website address to build awareness of the site and its offerings. *Online* advertising is also used to drive traffic through to the website using the following methods:

- Links from other sites – these can be general sites with a similar profile of users whom you are targeting. Special interest sites, such as the Formula 1 website, will provide more targeted opportunities.

- Advertising on Internet service provider (ISP) portals such as Wanadoo and Yahoo! These can also be targeted, as they have the demographic details of their subscribers and have details of their high traffic sites.

- E-mail advertising – using information gained from customer details or purchased as lists from many organizations.

- SMS messaging (using mobile phones) is not strictly an Internet medium but is often used in the same way, targeting people by sending text messages. Airtime providers use this a great deal to market their own services but are now providing lists of numbers to other organizations, specifically for targeting hard-to-reach groups such as young adults.

Ultimately, the type of web advertisement used will depend on the target audience, the media chosen and the degree of information/creativity needed and possible. The advertisements are created in one of the following ways:

- Banner advertising – These are the most common forms of advertising, appearing on linked sites, and offer the ability for the viewer to click through into the advertising organization's website. There are also e-banners that allow e-transactions to take place.

- Pop-up ads – Often used not to advertise but to arouse interest via use of a game or clip of a film. Encourages the viewer to leave contact details to allow contact at a later stage.

- Superstitals – These appear whilst pages are being downloaded and provide entertainment whilst that is taking place. British Airways inserted one on the download to the *Times* newspaper website. However, with the improved penetration of broadband, opportunities may be limited in the future.

- E-mail and SMS as detailed above, where a very specific message can be sent directly to the recipient.

ACTIVITY

Research these different types of Internet advertising and conclude in what circumstances your organization might use each of them.

The Internet, like other web-based media, is a powerful relationship management tool. All methods and media allow us to be very targeted or quite general in our approach, dependent upon the linked site or portal chosen to carry the advertising. Content can be personalized, so each user receives information and messages that are relevant to them specifically. All uses are very measurable in that we are able to monitor the degree of 'click through'. A high level of interaction can also be built in to engage the viewer, and the content is flexible and can be updated regularly – at a cost.

Remember that the Internet can be used to communicate with all stakeholders, not just customers.

QUESTION

How might you use the Internet to communicate with suppliers, employees or shareholders?

Launching the C3 family car, Citroen realized it would have to branch out beyond traditional media channels to target women with young children. It worked with media agency OMD to tie up an ad partnership with AOL Time Warner, which enabled it to use two formidable ad platforms – AOL and IPC media – to target its audience.

America Online launched a branded micro-site offering ideas and tips on getting the best day out to support the creative idea, 'Family Days Out'. IPC magazines also ran advertorials and produced its own guides for mums, which supported the micro-site.

The campaign was a huge success – 110,000 AOL members visited the Citroen-branded micro-site with AOL the primary driver of traffic.

QUESTION

How might Bluetooth (see Unit 3) be used to communicate with stakeholders other than customers?

Direct Response TV gives the customer two ways of communicating with the organization. Digital viewers can use the 'red button' option if advertisers in-build this function into their television advertising, which Renault did with the launch of the re-styled Megane. The red button led the viewer to more detailed information, lists of local dealers and an invitation to test drive. Non-digital viewers are offered a telephone hotline number to gain more information.

Sponsorship and hospitality

DEFINITION

Sponsorship is

A specialized form of sales promotion where a company will help fund an event or support a business venture in return for publicity.

Source: CIM

Organizations often sponsor events that get 'spin-off' publicity on news or other media, such as sports matches (kit or billboards) or community events. They might also choose events that have an association with their target audience, such as accounting and legal firms sponsoring classical concerts and opera, or FMCG brands sponsoring music festivals.

DEFINITION

Hospitality is

When a company entertains people who may or may not be their direct employees.

Typical corporate hospitality focuses on individuals and groups of people external to the company who may influence the future commercial success of the company concerned. Thus corporate hospitality can

focus on distributors, possible or actual customers, influencers who may play a part in recommending a product or service, legislators or other external people of importance to the company.

Source: sticky-marketing.net

Corporate hospitality is often linked to social events, such as concerts, or sporting events such as football matches. Large-scale hospitality programmes are run by specialist agencies at such events as Wimbledon or the Olympics.

ACTIVITY

Find out how your organization uses hospitality and recommend (and justify) improvements.

Personal selling

When one visualizes the *'sales person'* many people will call to mind some negative images of either an unhelpful and impolite sales assistant in their local supermarket or a brash and unrelenting hard-sell salesman, usually connected with cars or double-glazing. Both of these scenarios communicate to the customer – in these cases, very badly.

The most important feature of personal selling as a tool of communication is that it involves two-way interactive communications taking place. This makes it the single most valuable tool in relationship management. Personal selling can be used in different ways dependent upon who the customer is.

In consumer communications, personal selling can provide the confused consumer with additional information at the point of sale. Customer objections can be investigated, discussed and hopefully dispelled. The sales person can help the customer evaluate the alternatives and choose the product or service that is best for them. If this is carried out in an unpressured professional manner the customer will feel empowered to decide and valued as a customer.

In a B2B situation, the *success* of an organization can depend upon the relationships that its sales people have within the industry. Here, the sales person has more of a differentiating role to play, highlighting the benefits of his products/services over those in the competition.

Objections will still need to be overcome, probably with accompanying guarantees as the customer seeks foolproof solutions, which will reflect well upon him in a pressured business environment. More emphasis will be placed on the terms and conditions of the relationship and the level of after-sales service and support on offer.

INSIGHT

Cadbury is one of the best-known brands in the UK and is synonymous with chocolate. In order to communicate and develop its brand with customers and other stakeholders, it uses a variety of communications methods.

Key marketing communications tools used by Cadbury:

- Advertising
- Point of purchase
- Public relations
- Direct marketing
- Website
- Personal selling
- Exhibitions and events
- Packaging
- Sales promotions
- Café Cadbury
- Sponsorship (*Coronation Street*)
- Trade promotions
- Product placements
- Cadbury World – associated merchandise
- Field marketing
- Vending machines.

One recent addition to this impressive list has been the development of Café Cadbury and its entry into the expanding coffee house market. Positioned as a 'Chocolate Experience', the Cadbury cafés seek to extend the Cadbury brand even though direct sales through these outlets will be small. The objective, as reported by Mason (2000), is to keep the Cadbury brand high in the minds of the public and to maintain the quality and trust that the brand has evoked. Cadbury refers to this brand extension as part of its present marketing programme.

Source: Fill (2002)

QUESTION

Are there opportunities to use (or use more) personal selling in your organization? How about personal selling to internal stakeholders?

Direct marketing

Direct marketing is a medium that is changing rapidly and could become a more strategic tool in the future. At present most of the uses are tactical in their nature and are methods of generating short-term sales leads.

Direct marketing allows us to send a personalized message to a consumer, generating a one-on-one communication. It is possibly the most targeted method of communication available to us marketers, yet the one that is least welcomed by the recipient.

Direct mail can be a powerful communication tool, but where it is sent indiscriminately it can irritate people and be judged as 'junk mail'. Wastage can be reduced if the mail shots are targeted at the right people. For example, it is very annoying for existing customers to be sent details of a new 'introductory' offer that they cannot take up because they are not new customers.

Direct mail also brings the organization into contact with stakeholders other than customers. Due to the volume of paper consumed, much (or even most) of which ends up as waste, environmental groups are very negative about bulk mailing. The issue of junk mail also interests regulators, and most countries operate a system where individuals can 'opt out' of receipt. In the UK, this system is the Mailing Preference Service (MPS).

INSIGHT

Tesco's club card loyalty device is perhaps the most successful sales promotion of its day. The club card device was instrumental in Tesco overtaking Sainsbury's into the Number 1 Grocery Retailer slot and going on to build a gap that Sainsbury's have never been able to bridge.

However, the club card continues to reap rewards even now in the arena of direct marketing. By monitoring the volume, frequency and brand choice of shoppers, Tesco are able to target direct mail to their customers. This means they can promote not only goods in store but also other Tesco products such as insurance, credit cards, telephone networks and savings. It is now possible to leave your home, insured by Tesco, drive to the store in your car, insured by Tesco, pay for your shopping with a Tesco credit card, collecting reward points on your club card for family days out that you can ring people up on your Tesco network to tell people about!

Technology is enabling many changes within the direct marketing arena. We need to ensure that those changes allow us to use direct marketing techniques more sensitively in order to try to reduce negative perceptions of the medium in the minds of the consumer.

QUESTION

Amazon is able to 'recommend' to customers, as it knows their purchase and viewing history. How might this affect sales?

Technological advances mostly generate the changes that are occurring within direct marketing. With direct marketing the changes have been primarily concerned with the collection, and manipulation of data – namely customer data and databases. We can now collect much more data than ever before from many different sources. Digital technology and the ability to establish more two-way methods of communication mean we can now access and process many more pieces of information into intelligent useable data. We can buy lists of customers of certain demographic profiles and product usage that are of a higher quality in terms of their accuracy than ever before. We now need to use these advances to become more targeted in our approach.

The customers have also evolved and are using their power. More customers are using services to opt out of receiving direct mail by a variety of services that have evolved to rid them of this intrusion into their lives. It is now possible to remove one's name from mailing lists, express one's wish not to receive direct marketing telephone calls and to bin direct mail communications. It is also a legal requirement for organizations to offer customers an 'opt out' from mailing and third-party use of their data.

Sales promotion

DEFINITION

Sales promotion is another communications tool that marketers use. It is often described as
  A short-term tactical marketing tool that gives customers additional reasons or incentives to purchase. (CIM)

The incentive will be linked directly to the promotional objective. With an entirely new product the promotional objective will be to build awareness and the sales promotion objective will be to induce trial of the new product to turn trialists into end users. With products in the maturity stage of the product life cycle (PLC), the promotional objective will be to remind people of the product benefits, the sales promotion objectives will be to get them to buy more (3 for 2) and render them less able to switch brands.

Sales promotions can be used as a dual-purpose tool by targeting two different customer groups. Consumer promotions to encourage consumers to go and buy are referred to as *pull* strategies because the customer by demanding the product is *pulling* it through the distribution chain. Trade promotions targeting the intermediaries in the distribution chain are used to encourage the intermediaries (often wholesalers or retailers) to stock or recommend the product. This is known as a *push* strategy as the organization seeks to *push* the product through the chain towards the end user. By using a combination of *push* and *pull* it should be possible to have the product in store at the precise moment the customer demands it.

So the objectives of a sales promotion can be expressed in any (or all) of the following ways:

- **Encourage trial of product** – to overcome any negative perceptions, encourage brand switching.

- **Extend existing customer base** – by reducing the cost of brand switching.

- **Prompt customers to change brand**

- **Generate bulk buying** – your consumers will not brand switch if they have residual stock of your product.

- **Overcome seasonal dips in sales** – which may result in peaks and troughs smoothing out in time.

- **Encourage trade to stock product** – as they know customers are to be incentivized.

Consumer sales promotions usually offer temporary added value to the customer at the point of purchase. There are many different versions of sales promotions that are directed at consumers:

- Price reductions

- Coupons/money-off vouchers

- Entry to competitions/free prize draws

- Free goods

- X per cent free

- 3 for the price of 2 (or buy one get one free – BOGOF)

- Free samples or gifts

- Guarantees or extended warranties

- £x goes to y charity if you purchase

- Reward points/tokens against a free gift (e.g. air miles)

- Refunds or free gifts on a mail-in basis.

Sales promotions aimed at the trade include:

- Discount on bulk orders

- Free supplies

- Incentives (e.g. shopping vouchers for Marks & Spencer or a free alarm clock)

- Free prize draw competitions

- Deferred invoicing

- Merchandizing and display material.

Sales promotions have great value in relationship management, if used wisely. Consumer promotions may trigger the first step in the relationship – a customer switching to 'our' brand. Many of the sales promotion tools also concentrate on encouraging loyalty – a key component of relationship management.

Similarly, trade promotions are used at every stage of the supplier–customer relationship. Once again, they can encourage switching or loyalty. Sales promotions are used widely in modern supply-chain management approaches, where organizations form long-term relationships for mutual benefit.

Some sales promotions involve organizations other than the supplier and customer. Offering 'cheap flights' to customers who collect vouchers, for example, involves a travel agent and an airline in the promotion. This can lead to conflicts between the marketing objectives of each party involved.

INSIGHT

The Institute of Sales Promotion (ISP) is launching an accreditation scheme intended to protect consumers from dishonest promotional activity. Kellogg and Coca Cola have already signed up to the ISP Seal programme, and its trade body expects a number of its other members to follow suit in the run up to the launch. The seal is designed to reassure consumers that promotions, such as competitions and two for one deals, are properly run. In 2008, the ISP recorded a record 750 per cent rise in complaints about promotions that had a digital element. Any promotion that has been passed by the trade body's legal advisory service will be eligible to use the logo on its packaging and above the line marketing. It marks the first consumer-facing activity to be undertaken by the ISP.

Source: Marketing: 29.04.10

QUESTION

How can sales promotions be used with stakeholders other than customers

Coordinating the communications mix

Going back to the definition of the communications mix, we must remind ourselves that all the component tools should 'work together'. This causes a number of problems:

- In any communications campaign, however targeted it is at a desired audience, there will always be an 'accidental audience' of other stakeholders. These individuals and organizations were not the intended audience for the communication but will receive it, have opinions about it and possibly act on it (though sometimes not in the way intended).

- In any but the most tightly targeted campaign, the communication will have multiple audiences. Each different stakeholder audience will have different needs and expectations. Indeed, an individual stakeholder (an employee, for example) might belong to several stakeholder groups (employee, customer, trade union member, shareholder, etc.), and each of these roles comes with its own set of expectations.

The challenge for marketers is to accommodate these differing stakeholder needs and minimize the impact of any conflicting messages. This can be achieved in different ways:

- By having 'core messages' (perhaps about quality and service levels) that are common to all communications. These messages need to be carefully thought out and tightly controlled as part of the marketing planning and communications monitoring processes.

- Having a series of minor variations on these core messages, or 'supplementary messages' (that add to, but do not conflict with, the core messages), each biased towards a different stakeholder audience. These discrete messages can then be used in such a way as to minimize conflicts between the different messages that might be received by any individual stakeholder.

- Using media that are very closely targeted to an individual stakeholder audience. The targeted media include personal selling, direct marketing and the new technologies that can identify individual recipients of a communication and tailor it accordingly.

INSIGHT

When Kofi Annan asked Havas Worldwide to work pro bono for this campaign for Climate Justice, they did not hesitate. Global warming is one of the biggest issues facing the planet. The 'tck tck, tck' (www.timeforclimate-justice.org) was launched at the 56th Cannes Lions International Advertising Festival alongside Bob Geldof and Kofi Annan. The idea was simple, a movement rather than a campaign, but with a deadline, December 2009, and the United Nations climate conference in Copenhagen. The idea was to put pressure on the world's leaders to deliver binding, just and global agreement in Copenhagen. The most important element to the campaign was that it was open to third parties. Havas Worldwide wanted the campaign to become a movement that consumers, advertisers and the media would interact with and exploit. The British government gave the campaign their official support and asked the top 100 businesses and media personalities to give it their backing. The combined total of 'tck tck tck' action – the official website acts as an online petition reaching more than a million people, and the movement has been taken up around the world, from Oxfam's stunts in Central Park to Young and Rubicon producing a TV advert in Brazil. The movement gained wide international TV and press coverage. The partner companies include Virgin Radio, Yahoo!, iTunes, Google, Pernod Ricard, You Tube, USA Today, HSBC, Marks and Spencer and MTV.

Source: Campaign 9.10.09

INTERNAL CUSTOMER LOYALTY

The range of tools

The loyalty of the internal customer can be split into two components:

1. Loyalty to the organization: All organizations want staff who are loyal to them, as good staff (like good customers) are much cheaper to retain than to attract. There are also knowledge issues related to staff retention as, with prolonged service, staff accumulate a huge body of knowledge and experience that would be a significant loss to the organization, should staff 'defect' to a competitor.

2. Loyalty to the message: It is essential that all employees 'buy into' the core messages and values of the organization. This will help to minimize the problem of conflicting messages discussed in the previous section and improve overall standards of customer service.

Internal customer loyalty is an important issue because it helps to create and reinforce a long-term, win–win, relationship between the organization and the employee. This relationship begins as the employee is first attracted and recruited and can be initiated by the recruitment and induction processes. It then develops into the staff engagement and retention processes.
The staff engagement process has three main objectives:

1. Improving commitment to the organizations, and thus reducing staff turnover and increasing commitment levels.

2. This commitment translates directly into improved motivation levels and a higher level of productivity. This is good for the organization but might also lead to improved reward for the employee through bonuses and promotion.

3. The end result of this commitment and motivation is that the staff member becomes an advocate for the organization, selling it to prospective customers and employees.

Can the ladder of loyalty be related to staff, as well as customers

The following sections outline the range of tools that can be used to encourage employee loyalty and advocacy.

E-mail

E-mail can be used in the same way as direct mail with the communication adapted to become screen size and easy to print off. Attachments or hyperlinks to websites can further enhance the message although after many virus scares concerning unsolicited attachments, recipients are choosing to delete 'Spam' in droves without even opening the e-mail. However, the significant cost and time benefits of e-mail over postal methods especially on a global scale will continue to secure its future use.

While e-mail is the preferred internal communication tool in most organizations, many miss out on the 'internal marketing' opportunities that it provides:

- Staff can collaborate, even when 'on the move' by using mobile devices such as a Blackberry. This gives access not only to colleagues but also to resources on the organization's intranet (see below).

- Staff can be sent links to resources using 'really simple syndication' (RSS) feeds, which compile a reading list of hyperlinks, each with a brief description of the resource to which it links.

- Newsletters, containing information about the organization's activities, products and stakeholders, can be distributed by e-mail. These newsletters can even be compiled by the readers, using Wiki technology.

Do you receive 'engagement' e-mails from your employer? Compare and contrast these examples from your study group.

Intranet

An intranet is an information system that is used to communicate internally within an organization. This allows all employees within an organization, regardless of how many sites they are located at or the geographical location of those sites, to communicate almost instantaneously. This not only effectively negates the need for memos as we highlighted earlier but also allows for electronic transfer of any electronically held information such as reports, letters and data to be transmitted as attachments. The organizational address book allows users to select by name without putting in the whole e-mail address.

Intranets are powerful tools in relationship management, as they are only open to current relationship 'partners'. Like all digital media, the content viewed can be tailored or personalized by means of cookies (packets of data identifying the user) so that each viewer receives a personal communication.

Content can also be created by the users. The most common collaborative tools (collectively known as Web 2.0 tools) are blogs and wikis.

Blogs

A blog is an online diary. The blogger posts their views and opinions on a daily (or less frequent) basis, and the content is viewed 'backwards'. The blogger includes, in the content, resources such as graphics, pictures and sound and video clip, and also links to other web resources that are relevant to the topic(s) under discussion. The growth of a blog tends to be pretty controlled, as all the content is created or added by the individual blogger.

Unsurprisingly, the most common use for blogs in business is for employees (often senior managers or CEOs) to record their thoughts for the consumption of colleagues.

While the primary aim of a blog is for an individual to air their views and opinions, bloggers need to recognize that anyone posting a response to a blog comment expects (and deserves) to be listened to and treated with respect. Insincere or dismissive responses will only annoy them and can easily lead to a snowball of bad publicity.

Bloggers should also stick to what they know. For example, customers trying to use an industrial product (such as a machine tool) will appreciate tips and hints from the supplier's engineers. What they will not respond positively to is bland marketing messages or trumped-up claims. However, blogs should also be personal. Interspersing a blog on technical issues with the occasional comment about the blogger's kids or pets will give the resource a personality and engage the reader.

INSIGHT

The Seattle Children's Hospital uses a derivative of blogging software to allow users to create and update its events calendar. This does not look like a conventional blog, but the software is so easy to use that it makes old-fashioned content development packages obsolete.

INSIGHT

Direct2Dell provides a blog-based resource for the company's users to discuss issues and solutions. Although much less structured than the company's formal web content, this system is responsive and interactive.

INSIGHT

Blogs also have a role in education. Aaron Campbell, a teacher of English, has started his own blog 'The New Tanuki' for his EFL students. He finds that the 'linear' nature of a blog suits the way that learners develop but that its use of extensive hyperlinks suits the exploratory nature of learning.

Do not forget the 'internal' blog, though. What about using a blog to record modifications to software or to monitor the progress of an R&D project?

You can also, by the way, make a business out of a blog. If you do not believe me, check out 'The Bag Snob' (bagsnob.com) or 'Manolo the Shoe-blogger' (shoeblogs.com).

Other potential applications include:

- **CEO or executive blogs** – Boeing, Sun, GM, Edelman all have them. Keep stakeholders updated on your thoughts and plans, but be careful not to lose any potential competitive advantage.

- **Every employee** – Forrester Research analyst Charlene Li reckons the day is not far away when every new starter will be given a URL for their own blog as part of their induction package. They will be expected to record their experiences and impressions, as well as keep a record of development activities.

- **Company news** – The diary-like structure is ideal for 'what happened this week/month'-style records, as it is for scheduling social events or recording the results of marketing visits.

- **Audit notes** – Let the audit team and client blog issues and possible solutions (and get an audit trail of discussions, too). It is much more interactive, and less wasteful in terms of time, than a series of meetings.

- **Knowledge networking** – Users can advertise their specialist areas and offer online help to colleagues. Blogs are great for personal intranet pages. Wikis work better for teams and departments, as we will see.

- **New accounting standards** – Again, seeing issues develop along a time sequence is a logical approach and maintains an audit trail.

Blogs are relatively easy to control, as they grow fairly slowly and in a linear fashion.

ACTIVITY

Search for blogs that are relevant to your industry and evaluate them.

Wikis

A wiki is a relational database containing information that is all related to a common theme. While wikis contain similar content, resources and links to blogs, they tend to look more elaborate and professional. Blogs tend to be kept simple to reinforce their 'private and personal' nature.

Unlike blogs, wikis tend to grow exponentially, as the number of users grows, and their posted content multiplies. For example, Wikipedia, the online encyclopaedia 'written by its readers', has grown hugely since its 2001 formation. It now (March 2008) contains over 2.5 million articles in its English version.

INSIGHT

Wikipedia itself was born on 15 January 2001. Its first non-English offshoot (German) was established on March 16th of the same year, followed a few minutes later by Catalan. French Wikipedia followed a few days later, then in May came Chinese, Dutch, Esperanto, Hebrew, Italian, Japanese, Portuguese, Russian, Spanish and Swedish ... Wikis just grow and grow.

Other potential internal applications of wikis include the following:

- **Internal control and compliance issues** – Many organizations use wikis in areas of business that require collaboration. R&D is an obvious example, but what about the development of compliance standards? Think about how many meetings you need to get a change to an internal control policy approved!

- **Project team wikis** – this is an obvious one. Using a combination of blogs and a wiki makes any project easier to control. Microsoft does this, as does Boeing. The collaborative nature of wiki-building suits the way that projects work, and using a wiki encourages collaboration and communication.

- **Year-end wikis** – avoid all those tedious meetings and the duplication of effort when the auditors ask 15 different people for the same information.

- **Technical issues wikis** – for different accounting standards, tax, security, how the ERP system works (or does not), etc.

ACTIVITY

Make a list of specific ways your organization might use Web 2.0 tools to improve employee engagement.

Training

Training can be seen as a formal, often short-term process where the organization attempts to improve an individual's ability to perform a particular set of tasks. It can take place off or on the job or be a combination of both. Much management training is 'ad hoc' based on a specific training need identified in the appraisal process. Many organizations are moving to preferred suppliers for training in order to control cost and outcomes more closely. In this way the value-adding effect of training is increased.

'On-the-job' training from others can be effective if the existing employees have time to devote to the process and are themselves competent and know how to impart the necessary skills. Unfortunately these conditions are often not satisfied in practice; therefore, other methods such as simulations, class or laboratory-based training or off-site training may be more effective.

One development in the UK is competence-based training linked to a system of NVQs. The essence of competence-based training is that it assesses the ability of the trainee to carry out specified activities to prede-termined standards rather than concentrating directly on an individual's knowledge and understanding. This development can be seen as a conse-quence of the collapse of the traditional apprenticeship system and the uncoordinated proliferation of vocational qualifications. NVQs operate at five levels from basic training to professional level and provide the basis for national training targets specifying the proportion of young people and employees who will have obtained these NVQs by specified dates.

Whatever form of training or development is used it ought to be part of a systematic overall training system involving the following:

- Determining training needs

- Identifying training objectives

- Developing criteria against which to assess performance

- Developing methods to determine current levels of proficiency among potential trainees to enable the right people to be selected for training

- Making arrangements for the location, type and duration of the training

- Devising methods for carrying out the training and encouraging effective learning

- Monitoring the effectiveness of the training and comparing outcomes against criteria.

Regrettably much training is not subject to systematic planning, and careful evaluation is the exception rather than the norm. This implies that time, effort and money will be expended on training programmes without a clear understanding of benefit achieved as a result. The issue of how best to evaluate training should be considered before training begins. It is generally recognized that there are four levels at which training can be evaluated using the Kirkpatrick (1998) model:

- **Reaction** – evaluates how well the trainees liked the training.

- **Learning** – measures the extent to which trainees have learned the principles, facts and theories covered in the training.

- **Behaviour** – concerned with the extent to which behaviour changes as a result of the training.

- **Results** – considers what benefits (e.g. better quality, reduced costs) result directly from the training.

These levels will not necessarily be independent of each other, but each dimension represents a rigorous evaluation. When designing methods of evaluation, the most common approach is simply to measure outcomes at one or more levels after the training. The limitation of this design is that it makes it difficult to know whether the outcomes being measured are a result of the training or not. This can be overcome to an extent by measuring outcomes before and after the training: a pre/post-measure evaluation.

QUESTION

How could you measure the effectiveness of a training programme?

Most learn best when they are genuinely motivated to do so. Any training is most likely to be effective therefore, if the individual is involved in agreeing his or her training plan and in choosing the method or means by which the training is to be provided.

Information technology and particularly the Internet and intranet systems have provided new opportunities for training and development at relatively low cost Pritchard (2003), for example, notes the following:

- UK DIY products retailer B&Q (with 20,000 staff) uses computer-based training with locally run DVD-ROMS. B&Q also uses networked management tools to keep track of training progress.

- Car producer Ford uses e-learning powered by an intelligent search and retrieval system (Ford Learning Network). This allows all its 335,000 employees worldwide to access training material in a wide range of subjects from engineering to finance. It also contains a search facility to assist with work-related problems.

Support

Technical support

Staff need to feel that they have the right tools to enable them to work effectively. This is true whether we are talking about practical tools (machinery, PCs or telephones) or intellectual tools (knowledge, skills or contacts).

Specific examples of how staff can be provided with intellectual support for the technical aspects of their work include the following:

- IT helpdesks, so ICT equipment can be used to its full capabilities.

- FAQ sections on the organization's intranet, so staff can quickly find answers to technical problems.

- Knowledge networks, so staff can find out who the acknowledged experts are within the organization and approach them for advice and assistance.

QUESTION

How might Web 2.0 tools be used for technical support?

Management support

When trying to encourage staff to perform to their full potential, the art of good management is to encourage autonomy and creativity while still providing supervision, support and assistance. While most staff join an organization (or take a job) because of the organization (or job) itself, most staff who leave do so because of dissatisfaction with the organizational culture or individual manager with whom they have been working.

Appraisals

Appraisal of performance is a vital part of the HR cycle. Most appraisal systems should provide the individual with valuable feedback on their performance and focus on future development activities. Most schemes rely on a regular (perhaps annual or quarterly) meeting between the employee (appraisee) and his or her appraiser. The purpose of appraising may be seen as follows:

- Aiding technical, professional and management development

- Allowing a systematic follow-up of the results of staff development activities

- A source of motivation

- Enabling the achievement of rewards (such as promotion)

- Feeding into a wider reward system

- Increasing performance

- Helping achieve important organizational and individual objectives.

Other benefits are recognized as including:

- A mechanism to set objectives for the next period

- Identifying good prospects for promotion or transfer

- Developing psychological dependence on the manager

- Fostering an open atmosphere

- Developing relationships

- Enhancing corporate cultural norms.

In small firms, formal systems of performance appraisal are unlikely to exist, as judgements about performance will be made on the basis of personal observation and experience.

Irrespective of the organization, good managers should ensure these judgements are fed back to employees on a regular basis.

Many of the pitfalls associated with the selection interviews also apply in appraisal, including the following:

- A lack of preparation on either side

- An appraiser talking more than the appraisee and asking leading questions to which the answer is obvious, and important aspects may be left unexplored

- Appraisers being just as nervous as the appraisees

- Little or no appraiser training.

Appraisers can improve the quality of interviews considerably if they keep in mind the overall objective, which is to get an accurate idea of performance and improvement needs.

The first task is to try to overcome the rather unnatural circumstances of the formal interview and to encourage the applicant to relax and speak freely. To do this, the interviewer must keep the conversation flowing, while speaking no more than is necessary. By careful questioning the interviewer should bring out how well (or badly) the employee has matched the requirements of the job. The interviewer should always retain control of the situation.

Some factors present in effective appraisal systems include the following:

- Careful planning, which ensures the purpose and objectives of the system are widely understood.

- Skill in carrying out the appraisal interview.

- Selecting the most appropriate method of appraisal.

- Setting challenging targets that the appraisee can influence.

- Adopting a participative system that enables those being appraised to have a meaningful input to the system.

Good interviews are well prepared and conducted in an orderly and thorough manner.

Table 4.1 indicates some of the detailed considerations that an appraiser should take into account.

Table 4.1	Appraisal meeting issues

- Be properly organized and allow enough time.
- Make sure there will be no interruptions (divert telephone calls, etc.).
- Discuss issues of principle beforehand with senior manager and/or HR expert.
- Identify possible reasons for unusual performance, particularly if it is possibly 'below par'. (Problem recruitment, inadequate training or experiences, qualifications, etc.?) Check beforehand on the policy to address poor performance.
- Plan questions to be asked (they should be designed to probe performance and the training or development needs arising).
- Identify mechanisms to address individual training needs (e.g. refer to corporate training programme).
- Identify potential rewards for high performance (promotion policy, levels of salary increase, opportunity available for job moves).
- Identify opportunities for sideways development moves or job enrichment.
- Anticipate the information needed to meet likely questions from the appraisee.

The scheme must be consistent with the organization's reward and other systems, otherwise major problems will be caused if development activities identify one set of behaviours whilst others are rewarded in practice. Certain approaches will be adopted to make judgements and provide a basis for discussion in the appraisal interview, such as the following:

- Trait-orientated ratings of the individual on a number of personal-related dimensions, such as timekeeping and attitude towards work. A systematic appraisal of a subordinate's performance attempts to make inherent problems 'visible' and overcome them by focusing on the job rather than just the individual's personality. It attempts to be current rather than considering past experience.

- Result-orientated or 'performance appraisal' whereby appraiser and appraisee agree objectives and review progress of achievement accordingly.

- Some combination of both approaches.

Overell (2003) reports on research into employee appraisals and identifies that most large companies use such a system. This does, however, vary according to the industry (for instance in financial services, 80 per cent of employees have them compared with 50 per cent in retail). Private sector appraisals are conducted mainly to identify training needs, with evaluating performance secondary, and only 8 per cent of companies use appraisals for tackling poor performance. Surprisingly perhaps only 15 per cent of companies use appraisals to determine pay.

Overell also reports that, disturbingly, it was once found that in the UK's Civil Service the appraisal system was felt to discriminate against ethnic minority and disabled workers. (As a safeguard, management have since set up an independent assessor system, allowing staff a right of appeal.)

The question of who should appraise and when depends on determining the goal of appraisal and who is best placed to evaluate the employee's performance or needs against these. Managers often save up bad news rather than 'disciplining' staff at the time so that they will have 'ammunition' if necessary at the annual appraisal, even though this is inappropriate. Moves to more frequent appraisals run against the problem of time. Nevertheless, some managers do have weekly team briefings or individual discussions with staff as part of their ongoing managerial role that can be specifically aimed at assessing progress towards objectives.

Setting objectives as part of a performance appraisal involves agreement on SMART objectives (specific and challenging, measurable, but achievable, relevant and realistic and time-bound). A system of 'management by objectives' (MBO) is helpful if the employees are participants in their own objective setting. Otley's research into managers in the budget-setting process indicated that performance collapses if objectives have been set inappropriately. This means that appraisal of performance is potentially a very damaging activity for managers who treat it lightly or for organizations who do not consider the implications. This is particularly true of systems that apply pay to performance (PRP) based on appraisal interviews. These systems are treated with great suspicion by trade unions wary of unfair application and treatment.

The problems in coming to an accurate judgement of realistic objectives and then the rating of the employee against those objectives are the main cause of subsequent feelings of unfairness among the workforce and accusations of favouritism. Damage done to individuals selected as poor performers can spread as others sympathize.

Finally, a number of types of appraisals exist:

- **Self-appraisal** – This often takes place in preparation for a supervisor/appraisee meeting. This can save managerial time, but the value may be questionable (if the appraisee is too self-critical, or too lenient or critical incidents have been omitted).

- **Supervisor/appraisee** – Normally the person who allocates work and establishes priorities and standards appraises. In some cases, where there are many workers this may not be possible.

- **180-degree** – Often managers, especially those in project teams or matrix organizations and professional bureaucracies, do not 'know' the appraisee sufficiently well. To some extent, collecting anonymous or named views of colleagues can solve this. This can also be performed in the open groups session with the emphasis on first how the group performed and then the individuals' contribution (or the lack of it).

- **360-degree** – This is where the appraisee prepares feedback on the appraiser as well as getting 180-degree feedback from colleagues. Problems include potential conflicts, power, influence issues, time and bureaucracy.

Flexible working

Flexible structures

HR practices inevitably vary dependent upon the specific organizational size, culture and availability of specialist HR or personnel managers to support management in carrying out their duties. Organizational structures, particularly those engineered to achieve operational flexibility, are another important dimension impacting on HR practice. The need to respond to a fast-moving environment has led to organizations moving from traditional hierarchies to adopting more flexible organizational structures, including fluid matrix or project-based firms. Alongside these, virtual or networked firms have grown. Inevitably these nontraditional structures have presented new HR challenges and required managers to adapt traditional approaches to these local contexts.

HR thinking and practice need to evolve in responses to the challenges of flexibility and environmental uncertainty, specifically in the areas of the following:

- Planning horizons

- Staff appraisal where there may be no formal supervisor/subordinate reporting relations

- Remuneration strategies (see previous unit) where outputs are not easily attributable to individuals alone

- The structure of the workforce and the use of consultants and contractors

- Development, promotion and succession planning.

Flexible employment

There is nothing new about flexible employment, as casual work 'by the hour' or 'by the day' has long typified many industries enabling them to match the volume of labour exactly with the level of demand. Some management practitioners and theorists have accorded a renewed interest in workforce flexibility in recent years. The following reasons may explain why this should be so:

- Lower labour costs through operating at lower staffing levels

- Growing international competitiveness making flexibility a necessity

- Improved responsiveness to market changes

- Greater utilization of equipment

- Higher quality output

- Lower batch sizes tailored to specific market segments

- Organizational flexibility to adapt, innovate, diversify and divest

- Greater control of labour processes and costs.

Superficially an impression might emerge of widespread changes in employment patterns and working practices aimed at lowering wage costs and raising productivity. Blyton's (1992) review of research led him to the following conclusions:

- There has been a growth in various forms of flexibility in all areas, public and private sectors and manufacturing and services.

- Different types of flexibility are prominent in different sectors, and similar forms are being pursued for a variety of reasons.

- Flexibility agreements with unions have been important, but many of the changes have been introduced by unilateral management action.

Flexible employment also relates to trends in flexible working, such as working from home and 'hot desking'. While the key driver of such initiatives is often reducing the cost of premises, there are benefits to the employee as well as to the employer.

QUESTION

Why is flexibility attractive to staff?

Job redesign

Job redesign can be used to help develop individuals and groups within the workplace. Experience of different jobs increases an individual's understanding, skills and empathy with others.

The job characteristics model (as shown in Figure 4.1) sets out the links between characteristics of jobs, the individual's experience of those characteristics, and the resultant outcomes in terms of motivation, satisfaction and performance. The model also takes into account individual differences in the desire for personal growth and development (what Maslow called 'self-actualization').

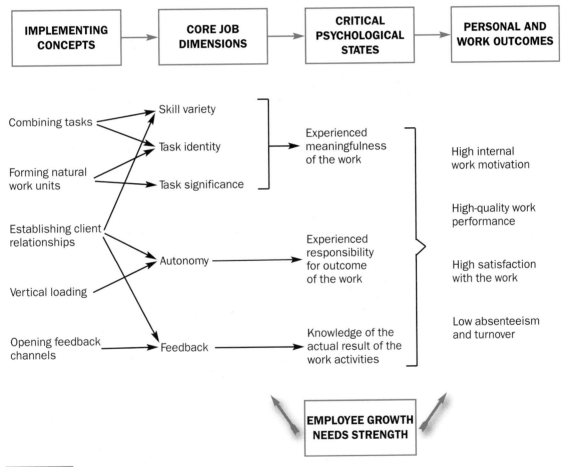

FIGURE 4.1 *Job characteristics.*
*Source: Hackman, J.R., Oldham, G., Janson, R. and Purdy, K. (1975) Califomia Management Review, **17**(4) p. 62. Reprinted with permission.*

The strength of the links in the chain set out in the model are determined by the strength of the individual's personal growth need, so the model does not apply to everyone. The heart of the model is the proposition that jobs can be analysed in terms of five core dimensions as follows:

1. Skill variety is the extent to which a job makes use of different skills and abilities.

2. Task identity is the extent to which a job involves a 'whole' and meaningful piece of work.

3. Task significance is the extent to which a job affects the work of other organization members or others in society.

4. Autonomy is the extent to which a job gives the individual freedom, independence and discretion in carrying it out.

5. Feedback is the extent to which information about the level of performance attained is related back to the individual.

These five core dimensions induce the three psychological states critical to high work motivation, job satisfaction and performance. These three states are defined as follows:

1. Experienced meaningfulness is the extent to which the individual considers the work to be meaningful, valuable and worthwhile.

2. Experienced responsibility is the extent to which the individual feels accountable for the work output.

3. Knowledge of results is the extent to which individuals know and understand how well they are performing.

Jobs that have high scores are more likely to lead their incumbents to the experience of these critical psychological states than jobs that have low scores. Expectancy theorists argue that all the three critical psychological states must be experienced if the personal and work outcomes on the right-hand side of the model are to be achieved.

Job rotation and secondments

Staff engagement can be encouraged, and new skills learnt by rotating between roles and departments. This is commonly done on 'fast-track' management training programmes but can work equally well for all staff.

The benefits of job rotation to the individual include the following:

- Less monotony in the nature of work

- A chance to experience different parts of the organization and to gain new skills

- A chance to see new opportunities and even to lobby managers for future career development opportunities.

Though the organization may be reluctant to encourage job rotation, due to the cost of retraining and the disruption caused, there are also significant benefits to be gained:

- Multi-skilled employees allow for more flexible working patterns and a far wider use of multi-disciplinary teams.

- Better career planning can be possible, as staff have a clearer idea of where they wish their career to develop

- Staff have greater engagement with the organization, and this leads to a reduction in staff turnover and improved productivity.

It is becoming increasingly common to allow staff to be seconded into other organizations. This is normally done in one of four 'directions':

1. Into a customer organization, to gain a better idea of customer needs and expectations.

2. Into a supplier organization, to understand how supply chain issues might be resolved.

3. Into service provider organizations, such as accountancy, legal or IT firms, to improve skills and strengthen relationships.

4. Into charitable organizations, as part of the organization's sponsorship and PR activity.

Gap years

Some organizations allow staff to take a 'career break', to further their personal development by means of activities that are not directly work-related. Such 'gap years' might allow a staff member to do the following:

- Travel widely and experience different cultures

- Do voluntary work with organizations that could not normally have access to senior staff

- Learn new skills, such as sports (scuba diving, martial arts), pastimes (cookery) or academic qualifications.

Team meetings

Team roles

You may be familiar with the work of Belbin from your study of organizational management. Belbin suggested that the perfect group (in this case team) has a number of members who collectively fulfil eight roles. It is not necessary for one individual to take on one role, as roles can be shared or individuals in smaller groups can take on more than one role. It is, however, important that all the roles are covered. Belbin's eight roles are shown in Table 4.2.

Table 4.2	Belbin team roles	
Role	**Typical features**	**Positive qualities**
1 Company worker	Conservative, dutiful	Organizational ability, practical common sense, hard work, self-discipline
2 Chairman	Self-confident, controlled	A capacity for treating all members on their merit, a strong sense of objectives
3 Shaper	Highly strung, outgoing, dynamic	Drive, and a readiness to challenge any ineffective behaviour
4 Plant	Individualistic, serious-minded, dynamic	Genius and imagination
5 Resource investigator	Extrovert, enthusiastic, curious	Contacts and networks, an ability to rise to a challenge
6 Monitor-evaluator	Sober, unemotional, prudent	Judgement, discretion and hard-headedness
7 Team worker	Mild, sensitive	An ability to build team spirit and solve disputes
8 Completer-finisher	Painstaking, conscientious	A capacity to follow through, a perfectionist

Meetings

Most managers seem to spend half of their life in meetings, so understanding how they work and how to make them more effective is very important.

DEFINITION

A meeting is a group of people coming together for the purpose of resolving problems or making decisions.

Meetings can be held for a wide range of purposes, but it is important that the purpose of the meeting is made clear to the participants in advance. If this is done, the meeting is more likely to be a success.

The most common reasons for holding a meeting are the following:

- To give advice or share information.

- To address a problem, grievance or complaint for resolution.

- To make a series of specific decisions about an issue.

- To generate creative ideas, for development outside the meeting.

- To present a proposal for discussion and approval.

When chairing a meeting, it is useful to summarize the objectives of the meeting at the beginning. This will help to focus the attention of the attendees on the job in hand. It may also be necessary to remind the meeting of its objectives at various stages, to stop the meeting drifting out of control.

There are two types of meetings at work:

1. **Formal meetings** – These take place in offices and conference rooms, and are planned and structured.

2. **Informal meetings** – These may just be colleagues bumping into each other in the corridor or at the coffee machine.

While this unit only considers formal meetings you must remember that, as Tom Peters said, 'most big problems in business are solved at the water cooler'.

The following (Table 4.3) are the main kinds of formal meetings that you might encounter at work. While there are many other types of formal meetings, they will often be similar to one of the below.

Table 4.3	Meeting types

Type	Characteristics
Board meeting A board meeting is a regular meeting between directors of a company. In some countries the power of the board is covered by company law	■ Often monthly ■ Normally in a regular venue such as a boardroom ■ Chaired by the Chairman or Chief Executive of the company – an elected officer
Committee meeting A group of people who have been delegated responsibility for specific tasks or areas of business	■ Meets regularly ■ Some committees are permanent ■ Some committees only meet until their task is completed
Working group Generally a fairly small group of people, given the responsibility of implementing the decisions of a committee, or exploring a particular aspect of a committee's work	■ Only exists for a short period ■ Has very narrow terms of reference ■ Reports back to committee
Public meeting A meeting held by the organization to brief the general public, including the media	■ One-off meetings ■ Deal with specific issues ■ Often arranged by the public relations department
Conference A large meeting at which several presentations on a topic are give to a group of delegates	■ Little opportunity for discussion ■ Delegates sometimes pay to attend ■ Delegates are normally given information in a 'delegate pack' to take away
General meeting A legal requirement in most countries, the annual (AGM) or extraordinary (EGM) meetings of shareholders are covered by company law	■ Allows shareholders to question directors ■ Considers appointment of auditors ■ Directors seek approval for plans or 'ratification' of past decisions
Client meeting A meeting with a customer or client to discuss aspects of the relationship between the two organizations	■ May be held on neutral ground ■ Often called to resolve disagreements
Project review meeting Regular meetings (see units 1–3) to brief participants in a project	■ Normally fairly brief ■ Well structured and minuted ■ Report progress ■ Seek authorization to proceed
Team briefing A meeting between a manager and a group of subordinates to pass on information	■ Often regular (weekly or monthly) ■ Fairly informal
Appraisal A periodic meeting between a superior and subordinate, to review progress and set objectives	■ Often governed by company policy ■ Normally minuted and records held by both parties ■ May be linked to salary increase

Table 4.3	Meeting types (*Continued*)
Type	**Characteristics**
Interview A meeting between a job applicant and one or more organizational representatives, normally including the manager of the recruiting department	■ Often short ■ May be part of an 'assessment centre'
Brainstorming An informal meeting to generate ideas	■ Often very unstructured ■ Requires careful control and minute-taking

FIGURE 4.2 *Meeting life cycle.*

A good meeting should have a beginning, a middle and an end. It should be carefully steered by the Chair through a series of stages. For a formal meeting, the life cycle may look like Figure 4.2.

INSIGHT

Compass Group PLC is a market leader in providing food and a range of selected support services to customers in the work place. Compass operates in 70 countries with more than 400,000 employees and generates annual revenue of approximately 11 billion GDP.

Norwich Union is the approved and preferred healthcare supplier and in order to promote and publicize the service to employees Compass undertook the following actions:

1. Regular internal communication to reinforce key messages and promote loyalty to wards Norwich Union. Employees were given key information on

process and procedures and advised of where they could obtain further information.

2. Free healthcare checks to encourage trail of the new healthcare service. This provided an opportunity for employees to meet Norwich Union staff and build up trust.

3. Internal publicity programme.

4. Social activities to improve face-to-face communications between Compass Group and Norwich Union and help to develop a long-lasting and mutually beneficial relationship.

INTERNATIONAL COMMUNICATIONS

The challenge of international markets

International marketing involves recognizing that people all over the world have different needs. Companies like Gillette, Coca-Cola, BIC and Cadbury Schweppes have brands that are recognized across the globe. While many of the products that these businesses sell are targeted at a global audience using a consistent marketing mix, it is also necessary to understand regional differences, hence the importance of international marketing.

Organizations must accept that differences in values, customs, languages and currencies will mean that some products will only suit certain countries and that as well as there being global markets – e.g. for BIC and Gillette razors, and for Coca-Cola drinks – there are important regional differences: for example, advertising in China and India needs to focus on local languages.

Just as the marketing environment has to be assessed at home, the overseas potential of markets has to be carefully scrutinized. Finding relevant information takes longer because of the unfamiliarity of some locations.

The potential market size, degree and type of competition, price, promotional differences, product differences as well as barriers to trade have to be analysed alongside the cost-effectiveness of various types of transport. The organization then has to assess the scale of the investment and consider both short-and long-term targets for an adequate return.

Adaptation versus standardization

Before becoming involved in exporting, an organization must find the answers to two questions:

1. Is there a market for the product?

2. How far will it need to be adapted for overseas markets?

The product must possess characteristics that make it acceptable for the market – these may be features like size, shape, design, performance and even colour. For example, red is a popular colour in Chinese-speaking areas. Organizations also have to consider different languages, customs and health and safety regulations.

Standardization

DEFINITION

Standardization: manufacturing, marketing or employing other processes in a standard way.

If a company offers a product, which is undifferentiated between any of the markets to which it is offered, then standardization is taking place. The great benefit of standardization is the ability to compete with low costs over a large output.

In most markets, however, there are many barriers to standardization. It is not difficult to think about the standard marketing mix for a product and how this might vary from one country to another. For example:

- **Product** – Tastes and habits differ between markets.

- **Price** – Consumers have different incomes.

- **Place** – Systems of distribution vary widely.

- **Promotion** – Consumers' media habits vary, as do language skills and levels of literacy.

INSIGHT

The over fifties are now in the majority in Japan, and their cultural influence and buying power have forced brands to snap out of their chronic fixation with youth. Nintendo designed the Wii with Japan's older generation in mind, recreating games such as tennis and golf for the living room. MTV, the stalwart of the 18- to 34-year old demographic is thinking of screening more Beatles than Backstreet Boys to woo 'the Dankai generation' baby boomers and bigger spending advertisers.

'Japan is shifting from a culture which values newness and youth to one in which people and things are valued more with the advancement of time' Dave McCaughan, McCann Worldwide's Asia Pacific strategic planning director.

This has not gone unnoticed by advertisers. Unilever is careful to avoid lingering on the age-slowing properties of its Dove Pro-age skin care range in its advertising. The latest campaign featured the 60-year-old singer and actress Ryoko Moriyama.

'The message isn't about giving women beautiful skin per se. And Ryoko is considered a particularly beautiful woman,' Naoko Ito, the associate planning director at Dove's agency, Ogilvy and Mather, Japan, explained. 'We want Dove to be a celebration of inner beauty first, outer beauty second.'

Moriyama neatly falls into the Dankai bracket. Born between 1947 and 1949, Japan's baby boomers have started to retire, hitting the mandatory retirement age of 60 years. Approximately 3.6 million more salaried workers will have retired by 2009.

Source: Campaign 14.03.08

QUESTION

What might the benefits and disadvantages be, to the organization, of standardization?

Differentiation

DEFINITION

Differentiation: the process of making products or aspects of the marketing mix different so as to appeal to different markets.

With differentiated marketing, an organization will segment its overseas markets and offer a marketing mix to meet the needs of each of its markets.

QUESTION

What might the benefits and disadvantages be, to the organization, of differentiation?

Adaptation

DEFINITION

Adaptation: the process of making small changes to a standardized marketing mix to make it more relevant to local markets.

The success of many products in international markets has come about because marketers have successfully adapted their marketing mix to meet local needs.

To a large extent, the standardization/adaptation dilemma depends upon an organization's view of its overseas markets and the degree to which it is prepared to commit itself to meeting the needs of overseas customers. There are three main approaches that can be applied:

1. **Polycentrism** – With this marketing approach, a business will establish subsidiaries, each with its own marketing objectives and policies, which are decentralized from the parent company. Adaptation takes place in every market using different mixes to satisfy customer requirements.

2. **Ethnocentrism** – Overseas operations are considered to be of little importance. Plans for overseas markets are developed at home. There is little research, the marketing mix is standardized and there is no real attention to different customer needs and requirements in each market.

3. **Geocentrism** – Standardization takes place wherever possible and adaptation takes place where necessary. This is a pragmatic approach.

A confectionery and soft drinks manufacturer like Cadbury Schweppes typically produces a range of standard items that are sold throughout the globe using similar marketing mix. However, differences may occur in such aspects as distribution channels and pricing, as well as advertising in languages that are relevant to particular cultures. In addition such a company would produce some products which cater to particular tastes and which are relevant to particular cultures. New products might then be tested in a regional area before consideration of which other areas of the globe to roll out that product to.

ACTIVITY

Make notes about how you might need to change the marketing and communications mix of one of your organization's products or services, if you were to offer it to another (very different) country.

Culture, religion and protocols

National cultures

National cultures can be described according to the analysis of Geert Hofstede. These ideas were first based on a large research project into national culture differences across subsidiaries of a multinational corporation (IBM) in 64 countries. Subsequent studies by others covered students in 23 countries, elites in 19 countries, commercial airline pilots in 23 countries, up-market consumers in 15 countries, and civil service managers in 14 countries.

Hofstede found five dimensions of culture in his study of national work related values:

- **Small vs. large power distance** – The extent to which the less powerful members of institutions and organizations expect and accept that power is distributed unequally. Small power distance countries (e.g. Austria, Denmark) expect and accept power relations that are more consultative or democratic. People relate to one another more as equals regardless of formal positions. Subordinates are more comfortable with and demand the right to contribute to and critique the decision making of those in power. In large power distance countries (e.g. China) less powerful accept power relations that are more autocratic and paternalistic. Subordinates acknowledge the power of others simply based on where they are situated in certain formal, hierarchical positions. As such, the Power Distance Index Hofstede defines does not reflect an objective difference in power distribution but rather the way people perceive power differences. In Europe, Power Distance tends to be lower in Northern countries and higher in Southern and Eastern parts. There seems to be an admittedly disputable correlation with predominant religions.

- **Individualism vs. collectivism** – Individualism is contrasted with collectivism and refers to the extent to which people are expected to stand up for themselves and to choose their own affiliations or alternatively act predominantly as a member of a life-long group or organization. Latin American cultures rank among the most collectivist in this category, while the USA is one of the most individualistic cultures.

- **Masculinity vs. femininity** – Refers to the value placed on traditionally male or female values (as understood in most Western cultures). So called 'masculine' cultures value competitiveness, assertiveness, ambition, and the accumulation of wealth and material possessions, whereas feminine cultures place more value on relationships and quality of life. Japan is considered by Hofstede to be the most 'masculine' culture, Sweden the most 'feminine'. Anglo cultures are moderately masculine. Because of the taboo on sexuality in many cultures, particularly masculine ones, and because of the obvious gender generalizations implied by the Hofstede's terminology, this dimension is often renamed by users of Hofstede's work, e.g. to quantity of life vs. quality of life. Another reading of the same dimension holds that in 'M' cultures, the differences between gender roles are more dramatic and less fluid than in 'F' cultures.

- **Uncertainty avoidance** – Reflects the extent to which members of a society attempt to cope with anxiety by minimizing uncertainty. Cultures that scored high in uncertainty avoidance prefer rules (e.g. about religion and food) and structured circumstances, and employees tend to remain longer with their present employer. Mediterranean cultures and Japan rank the highest in this category.

- **Long- vs. short-term orientation** – Describes a society's 'time horizon,' or the importance attached to the future versus the past and present. In long-term oriented societies, values include persistence (perseverance), ordering relationships by status, thrift, and having a sense of shame; in short-term oriented societies, values include normative statements, personal steadiness and stability, protecting one's face, respect for tradition, and reciprocation of greetings, favours, and gifts. China, Japan and the Asian countries score especially high (long-term) here, with Western nations scoring rather low (short-term) and many of the less developed nations very low; China scored highest and Pakistan lowest.

These cultural differences describe averages or tendencies and not characteristics of individuals. A Japanese person for example can have a very low uncertainty avoidance compared to a Filipino even though their 'national' cultures point strongly in a different direction. Consequently, a country's scores should not be interpreted as deterministic.

Language and symbols

Language

According to Forrester Research, 'Web users are three times more likely to make purchases at sites that are presented in their native language.' The Dell computer company recognizes this. Its 'Premier Pages' websites, built for its business clients, are available in 12 languages. Localization reflects not only the native language but the local norms of weights and measures, time, currency and other cultural issues.

INSIGHT

One example of localizing is Nike, a worldwide brand. Nike has a site that is intended for an American audience, Nike.com. Then there is also Nikefootball.com. This site was created specifically so that Nike could capitalize on the popularity of the Euro 2000 soccer championships. The website is available in English, French, Spanish, Italian, Swedish, German, Portuguese and Dutch.

Soccer fans represent such a large market that it was well worth the expense to attract them. While both Nike sites can be accessed worldwide, they have different objectives and intended audiences.

But simply translating your English-language or other native language site will not make it global or multiculturally correct. Successful multicultural net communication, essential to creating an authentic global presence, is often about nuance. National pride in culture and language must always be part of web thinking, strategy and content. It is, for example, a grave cultural error to assume a phrase as simple as 'home page' is universally understood. In Spain, home pages are called 'pagina inicial' – literally the first page. In France, it's 'page d'accueil' – the welcome page.

A few years ago, Anderson Consulting studied electronic commerce and travel services and collected travel brochures. It discovered that while African and German brochures stressed adventure and danger, the US brochures emphasized nature and family. In short, they appealed to consumers in different ways.

Another cultural aspect which affects website design is colour. Company officials at Dell quickly realized they had made the mistake of surrounding most of the site's content with black borders, a sign of negativity or death in many cultures. The use of black in graphics and backgrounds is very popular in the United States, but the colour has sinister connotations in Asia, Europe, and Latin America.

These examples illustrate the difficulty of translating text from one language to another and conveying the original sense and content so that it is acceptable across cultures. There are other aspects of web design which can be both beneficial and also need careful use.

Symbols

Of course, language is just one issue that global e-commerce strategies must cover. As Dell found out, international sites must be designed with a knowledge of local culture. Just as using the wrong colour can be bad for business, carelessly chosen icons can be especially dangerous. That is because even those commonly used in the UK or USA may have no relevance in other countries. In most countries, for example, you can forget about using mailboxes and shopping carts. Users in European countries do not take their mail from large, tubular receptacles, nor do many of them shop in stores large enough for wheeled carts. The icon for the American mailbox does not convey to citizens of other countries the idea of sending mail. A more universally recognized icon is an envelope.

One aspect of functionality, which relates to globalization, is navigation within a website. A number of icons integral to commonly employed software have become de facto standards for indicating certain functions in software. Examples of these are the icons for folders, printers, bold, italics, underlines, arrows for forward and back. Beyond this small number of common icons, there are no universally accepted or adopted images.

Europeans understand the universality of graphical communication – long ago, they replaced 'hot' and 'cold' with red and blue dots on the taps in places such as international airports.

INSIGHT

A global leader will encounter diversity not only in the people that he or she leads but in the places they are led and in the cultures they make up. Far from shying away from this diversity, the successfully global leader will understand and value it and ensure that the organization functions well within diverse conditions. HSBC recognizes the importance of diversity and has used it as an advertising tool. The latest HSBC television advertising campaign celebrates cultural diversity across the world and points out the danger of ignorance. It then goes on to establish itself as an informed, culturally aware, organization that has embraced cultural diversity and made it part of its business ethic. Whether this is true or not is up to the consumer to decide. The advert concludes with the words 'The world's local bank', a clever slogan, which portrays HSBC as a globally aware organization that recognizes localized cultural values.

QUESTION

Look at your organization's logo. What might the colours and symbols used mean to different cultures?

Availability of technology and media

One key concern for global marketing is the choice of technologies. Many countries still have very low penetration rates of broadband Internet services or mobile telephones (particularly 3G), so campaigns using these media should either be avoided or adapted to suit locally available technologies.

While television is felt to be the most all-pervasive medium, there are still many parts of the world where television ownership is low. In such environments, organizations often have to revert to less 'modern' media such as cinema and billboards.

Ensuring consistency of key messages

When we looked, earlier, at the need to coordinate the communications mix, we came to the following conclusions:

- In any communications campaign, however targeted it is at a desired audience, there will always be an 'accidental audience' of other stakeholders. These individuals and organizations were not the intended audience for the communication but will receive it, have opinions about it and possibly act on it.

- In any but the most tightly targeted campaign, the communication will have multiple audiences. Each different stakeholder audience will have different needs and expectations. Indeed, an individual stakeholder (an employee, for example) might belong to several stakeholder groups (employee, customer, trade union member, shareholder, etc.), and each of these roles comes with its own set of expectations.

In a multinational campaign, these issues are even more relevant. The solutions are pretty much as before.

The challenge for marketers is to accommodate these differing stakeholder needs, and minimize the impact of any conflicting messages. This can be achieved in different ways:

- By having 'core messages' (perhaps about quality and service levels) that are common to all communications. These messages need to be carefully thought out and tightly controlled as part of the marketing planning and communications monitoring processes.

- Having a series of minor variations on these core messages, each biased towards a different stakeholder audience. These discrete messages can then be used in such a way as to minimize conflicts between the different messages that might be received by any individual stakeholder.

NEW TECHNOLOGIES AND STAKEHOLDER RELATIONSHIPS

The technological environment

The beginning of the twenty-first century has been interesting for the number of hundredth birthdays, including that of the first powered flight and the original development of brands such as Ford. Mass air travel and mass ownership of cars have altered society.

In the twenty-first century, convergent information and computer technologies will transform society. The Internet was originally conceived as a technical solution to a military planning problem: how to maintain communications after a nuclear attack. With commercial and consumer access to broadband, this technology has moved far from the uses originally conceived for it. The Internet is rewriting ways of conducting business in both the B2B and the B2C sectors. The development of digital cameras embedded in mobile telephones is adding yet another dimension to people's ability to communicate.

The marketer needs to interpret these developments creatively and imaginatively. For example, the impact of the Internet on book sales is not uniform. Some directories and reference books have, in effect, ceased to exist as people gain this type of reference information directly from the Internet. We may well be happy to buy the latest blockbuster online from

Amazon. However, the book addict is looking for a shopping *experience* and specialist shops are adapting to this, hence leading to trends such as coffee shops within bookshops to provide the right atmosphere and give shoppers an offline experience, the real joy of book buying.

Of all the aspects of the technological environment, none has changed as rapidly as communications technology. Mobile phones, the Internet, cable television and media messaging mean that we can now contact pretty much anyone, pretty much anytime.

This leads to huge challenges for marketers, for example:

- Word-of-mouth on new products can grow exponentially. Viral marketing means that a weak product can be 'found out' in a matter of hours, while a strong product can 'stock out' in the same period.

- On the Internet, your nearest rival is only 'one click' away. Customers are now less loyal, both to products and retailers than they have ever been. Price comparison takes seconds, feature comparison a few seconds more.

- To combat the 'fickle' nature of online shoppers, organizations are now concentrating on creating a 'digital footprint' by means of Web 2.0 tools (blogs and wikis) and by creating online communities through social networking sites such as MySpace. There are also business equivalents, such as Linkedin (where your authors 'live') to aid B2B networking.

INSIGHT

'Race Online 2012' is a government-backed campaign promoting the benefits of the Internet to the socially excluded. According to government statistics 10 million adults in the UK have never used the Internet and 4 million are 'socially excluded' from the web. Of these 4 million, 39 per cent are over the age of 65 years.

In its Digital Britain report, the government encouraged public service broadcasters to create content that promoted digital participation. Race Online 2012 will inform people that they could save an average of £560 a year by shopping and paying their bills online. The campaign backed by BT, Channel 4, Microsoft and Age Concern working with local authorities to raise awareness of the benefits of online access. The project will run alongside work by a consortium led by Ofcom also promoting digital participation.

ACTIVITY

Research how communication has changed over the last 50 years. What are the implications of this for marketing organizations.

Virtual conferencing

Web conferencing as a communication service has come of age, with many companies adopting it for crucial meetings with clients, analysts and the press. It is fast becoming a key factor in cutting costs and improving operational efficiency for many organizations. They have started accepting the enormous possibilities opened by this service.

The biggest advantage of web conferencing is that it is a virtual conferencing tool that enables you to productively and cost-effectively engage in your most important business with just a phone and a web browser. Unlike audio conferencing involving only voice communication, and video conferencing, which requires considerable investments, web conferencing acts as a virtual meeting place by sharing both voice and data of any kind simultaneously to multiple users at multiple locations.

Its features include presentation sharing, document sharing, file transfer, web browser sharing and white boarding (allows users to write and draw on an unlimited number of shared pages that can be saved and printed).

Web conferencing today has evolved from being a hi-tech tool for conducting virtual meetings to a business tool catering to different stakeholders. Some of the commonly used web conferencing applications are in sales and marketing conferences, training programmes, forecasting and reviews, software demos, software testing, product launches, global meetings and business development.

INSIGHT

Seeing an increasing demand for alternatives to traditional in-person business meetings, Internet portal Yahoo! Inc. launched new Internet broadcasting packages that will be available through the broadband services unit of its business communications division.

The Sunnyvale, California-based company avoided mentioning the events of Sept. 11, but said that with travel and meeting costs rising and the recent travel restrictions, it is introducing Virtual Conference services and launching an Executive Communications Center.

'Yahoo!'s solutions will allow companies to continue vital communications that were centered around large scale meetings and maintain critical and focused outreach to customers, sales forces and business partners,' said Jim Fanella, senior vice president of Yahoo!'s Business and Enterprise Services division.

It is also a step in the direction of monetizing the franchise, which Yahoo! has been working hard to do in the face of a decline in Internet advertising. It recently upgraded its other corporate offerings, for example, and recently launched two new fee-based packages at its GeoCities unit – GeoCities Pro and GeoCities Webmaster.

Yahoo! said the Virtual Conference solution combines audio, video, informational slides synched to presentations and a browser to view other meetings associated with the same conference; interactive tools for polling, question and answer, document sharing and audience surveys; registration, live attendance tracking and post event reporting on attendees; and archiving and hosting.

Source: Internetnews.com

ACTIVITY

Make a list of the ways your organization might use virtual conferencing to communicate with different stakeholders.

SMS

Text messaging is most widely used by airtime providers to try to get their customers to utilize more-paid-for services (such as latest football scores). It is probably the most immediate personalized method of direct mail, especially to the ever-evasive youth market. The issue at present is that this form of communication is seen as intrusive, and more creative ways of producing tailor-made messages are required for the consumer to see the benefit.

There are a number of attributes that SMS has that make it valuable to marketers, attributes that not only allow it to enhance existing practices but also to open up a whole new set of opportunities (see Table 4.4).

These attributes allow for a number of applications in different marketing contexts. The approach here is to define marketing contexts, identify

Table 4.4	SMS attributes
Attribute	**Notes**
Global reach	Mobile phone penetration and SMS usage among mobile phone users is high and growing fast. The cost of sending an SMS to the guy in the next street is the same as that of sending one across the globe.
Low cost	The cost of interaction using SMS is low in comparison to mail and telephone. Unlike e-mail and the Web, SMS is priced by the number of messages sent and not by bandwidth usage.
Always on	This is one of the biggest differentiators of SMS. It is always on, in the pocket of the user. The user is almost always alerted to its arrival at the instant of delivery. And the user can also respond instantly.
Discreet	Although SMS is always on, unlike a phone call, it allows the user the option to view the message at a later point. It is messaging *sans* conversation, and hence that much less intrusive, and can remain completely private.
Instant delivery	Delivery of SMS messages is instant, making it an ideal medium for alerts and timed notifications.
Existing infrastructure	SMS piggybacks on existing mobile infrastructure and for the user requires an existing mobile device.
Interactivity	SMS allows interactivity of text-chat. The interactivity can be person–person or person–program wherein the user interacts with an application.
Human touch	The short-text nature of an SMS message makes it nearly impossible to distinguish between the feel on one generated by a human and one auto-generated by software.
Storage	SMS messages can be saved till the time the user wishes to delete them. This feature, combined with the always-on aspect to SMS, makes it possible to send content that needs to be saved and used further.
Instant consumption	Unlike mail and e-mail, SMS messages have a low propensity to pile up and remain unread. They will usually get read as soon as they are received.
Personalization	Due to the short-text limitations, personalization is relatively uncomplicated but each interaction can be unique to that user.
Stable identifier	A person's mobile number is likely to be used only by that person, the only one being used by that person and not be changed frequently.
Confirmation	It is possible to get an automatic delivery confirmation of an SMS message with a date–time stamp.
Content	The content that can be transmitted is restricted but, with menu-driven applications, one can deliver a surprisingly wide array of interactive content.
Run applications	SMS is seen as a fun, personal interactivity tool. A host of information and entertainment-based applications have been devised, including games, dating, quizzes, etc.

SMS applications and tools and finally put the tools within context to show the full opportunity of SMS for marketers.

When using the different communication media, the marketer works within different contexts. The context may be that of a sales promotion, wherein the use might be seen primarily as a response device to a contest, or that of customer service wherein it may be seen as a device for logging requests and complaints, or branding or many others.

Within each context a mix of media is used for different functions. One may use mass media for awareness building, combined with direct mail and e-mail to a database of customers, with telephone, mail, web-form and SMS response, SMS reminders and payment through cash, credit card or premium-priced SMS. Table 4.5 shows some marketing contexts and the communication needs of each.

Table 4.5	Marketing contexts and communication needs	
Context	**Description**	**Communication need**
Mass awareness of brand	Rich content delivery to a mass audience to create awareness and influence attitude and behaviour.	Reach and rich content are key requirements.
Direct marketing	Direct delivery of marketing content to individuals, with a specific response or action in mind.	Penetration of the delivery medium should be sufficiently widespread in target audience.
Relationship management	Differentiated services/content delivered to customers. Recognition of valued customers and personalization.	Personalization, premium services, alerts and notifications, easy response, etc.
Brand interaction	Create a set of interactive information and entertainment services around a brand that the target can experience.	Information and entertainment applications; interactivity.
Market research	Question-answer or poll-type interaction to a select set of customers for market research.	Low-cost reach, permission and response mechanism.
Campaign/sales promo	One-off or campaign of activities for a specific short-term objective.	Reach, interactivity, response, entertainment, etc.
Workforce management	Information send-receive within a workforce management setting.	Security, request-delivery of specific content, integration with other productivity tools; alerts and notifications, etc.
New products/services	Development of new products and services for customers to interact with and consume. Also act as a strategy to tap new markets or to extend branding opportunities.	Value-added applications, information services that create and satisfy new and existing needs.

Table 4.6	Uses of SMS in marketing	
Tool	**Notes**	**Example**
Content pull	Content in the form of an SMS message is pulled by user to mobile phone.	User requests account balance update.
Content push	A message is pushed to a user's phone. It may be a marketing message or useful information or a blend.	Bank sends out a message informing a customer of their new Internet banking service.
Alert/reminder	Differs from a message push because the purpose is alert, not content delivery.	Bank alerts account holder of overdue credit card payment.
Interaction	Tool for multiple message interaction between user and firm.	User who is unwilling to take a call interacts with a customer service rep over SMS to supply details of a problem and get a solution.
Response	Use as a response device to a stimulus provided by another medium.	Customer responds to promotional competition offering a prize for a correct response to a question.
Fulfilment	SMS coupons/tickets/vouchers can be used as mobile-based fulfilment devices.	Winner of the competition receives an SMS coupon that can be redeemed for a free CD or can be flashed to allow free entry to a concert.
Transaction	Premium-priced SMS can be a method of effecting a payment.	User pays for a CD by sending a request to the mobile operator to bill him the required amount. Operator sends an SMS receipt, which can be displayed at the counter as proof of payment.
Entertainment	Games, quizzes	User plays a branded SMS quiz; marketing messages informing the teenager about a sale at the local jeans store are flashed between rounds. The message can be stored and displayed for a 10 per cent discount.
Novelties	Ringtones, logos, novelty messages	User downloads the theme song of a movie as a ringtone, sets a new screen logo and sends out novelty messages as greetings to friends.

While one can argue that SMS is basically about messaging and every SMS application is a variant of the same fundamental, the different variants do throw up many interesting options (Table 4.6).

ACTIVITY

Re-read the sections on 'e-distribution' and 'Bluetooth' in Unit 3.

VoIP

Voice over Internet Protocol (VoIP) is a communications protocol (set of rules and procedures) optimized for the transmission of voice through the Internet. It is sometimes known as IP Telephony, or Internet Telephony. It allows users to hold conversations alongside data transfer across any broadband connection, thus eliminating the need for a separate telephone line (and bill!).

While VoIP can facilitate multimedia communication between parties (who may be any stakeholder) it does rely on both parties having access to (and having downloaded and installed) VoIP technology.

Economic sustainability

The argument used to justify the introduction of any new technology is 'it will reduce costs'. But is this true? Certainly technology, and particularly that related to information systems, has the *potential* to reduce costs through reductions in staff levels (as we automate processes that previously were manual) or the reduction in overheads (such as office or data transport costs). However, if we try to assess the real cost impact of these technologies, quite often we find that the direct cost reductions have been more than offset by additional costs elsewhere (in support services such as administration or IT, for example).

The other problem with using technology to reduce cost is that everyone else is doing it, too! As soon as such technology becomes the norm in our industry, someone will pass part (or all) of the cost reduction on to the customer in terms of reduced price. Others will follow suit, and soon every competitor matches the new price level, and any impact on profitability is lost.

If we cannot look to cost reductions for an increase in economic sustainability, then what about the benefits of technology? Perhaps the greatest potential impacts are in the areas of customer and employee relations:

- From the point of view of the customer, many of the benefits of technology manifest themselves in improved customer satisfaction. This should lead to improved loyalty, a higher level of business and therefore increased profits.

- Technologies, if used wisely, should increase staff engagement. This should lead to reduced staff turnover, improved motivation levels and improved productivity. This, in turn, should result in improved profits for the organization.

Ecological sustainability

CSR

Corporate social responsibility (csr) is a concept whereby organizations consider the interests of society by taking responsibility for the impact of their activities on customers, suppliers, employees, shareholders, communities and the environment in all aspects of their operations. this obligation is seen to extend beyond the statutory obligation to comply with legislation and sees organizations voluntarily taking further steps to improve the quality of life for employees and their families, as well as for the local community and society at large.

The practice of CSR is subject to much debate and criticism. Proponents argue that there is a strong business case for CSR, in that corporations benefit in multiple ways by operating with a perspective broader and longer than their own immediate, short-term profits. Critics argue that CSR distracts from the fundamental economic role of businesses, others argue that it is nothing more than superficial window-dressing, still others argue that it is an attempt to pre-empt the role of governments as a watchdog over powerful multinational corporations.

In 1995, the oil company Shell set a precedent for future behaviour when it decided to reverse its decision to dump the oil storage platform, Brent Spar, into the sea. This early example of CSR illustrated how a moral duty to do 'the right thing' replaced more reasoned, scientific criteria for making decisions.

Over 10 years on, we see that notions of corporate social responsibility are influencing business behaviour like never before. Food companies are reducing the fat content of their products, and drinks manufacturers are telling their customers to drink more responsibly. Retailers withdraw products from the shop floor, from bullets to sun tan lotion, in an effort to show moral responsibility. Companies send their employees on diversity training courses and encourage them to learn ethical codes of conduct. Internationally, multinationals pull out of infrastructure projects and emerging markets on the grounds of CSR. Elsewhere, virtually all corporations today strive to be more transparent and accountable, improve social, environmental and ethical performance and engage in better stakeholder relations.

CSR in action

Founded in 1997, American Apparel originally supplied plain wholesale T-shirts to a range of US clients. Having relocated its factory from Mexico to Los Angeles, it began promoting its product as 'Made in downtown LA-sweatshop free'. When it moved into retail in 2002, something about its bright, logo-free basics struck a chord with consumers, and the company began an international expansion programme. The success of American Apparel can be partly attributed to Don Charney, the founder who deliberately made his droll 1970's persona part of the brand's appeal. The advertising is grainy, off focus, featuring young attractive women in provocative poses wearing the brands clothing. American Apparel has succeeded in being both politically correct and incorrect at the same time.

The stores are minimalist white spaces, as well as lined with T-shirts, underwear, abbreviated skirts and hooded sweatshirts, are photographic galleries featuring urban imagery from the 1970s and photographs of urban rebels that inspire shoppers to get the look.

The company produces a million unit a week at its seven-floor garment factory in Los Angeles. It pays its 2,500 plus workers about US$13 an hour, well over the minimum wage. It claims that constant reinvention to create high customer demand, aligned with sheer volume of output, make the profit margins practical. Charney's strategy is vertical integration, which brings designers, marketers, cutters, sewers and knitters together under one roof – reduces costs and improves quality control. American Apparel's anticorporate values have given it a successful positioning strategy and its commitment to sweatshop-free production continues to drive its international expansion.

Source: Turngate (2008)

Carbon footprint

The biggest impacts that organizations can have on their carbon footprint are as follows:

- Reducing the amount of energy consumed by office buildings and processes.

- Reducing the use of fossil fuels in travel and logistics.

The former can be impacted by the design of 'greener' offices and the use of more environmentally acceptable energy generation methods, the latter, by the use of alternatives to travel (such as virtual conferencing) or reductions in the amount of fuel used (by using 'greener' cars such as Toyota's Prius or by simply travelling fewer miles).

INSIGHT

UPS, the world's largest package delivery company, today announced that it has completed the installation of technology that will significantly reduce the number of miles driven by its familiar brown package cars on Sacramento roads, subsequently reducing fuel consumption and emissions.

The new technology, which UPS calls package flow technology, consists of software and hardware that enable the company to map out shorter and more efficient routes for drivers. The new technology already has been implemented in UPS's Shore Street facility.

Each year, UPS drivers log more than 4.5 million miles on Sacramento-area roads. Based on initial results, package flow technology will reduce the number of miles driven each year in Sacramento by as much as 265,000 miles, saving more than 30,000 gallons of fuel and emitting 288 fewer metric tons of CO_2.

'Reducing fuel consumption and vehicle emissions is especially critical in Sacramento because the American Lung Association ranks this area as one of the most ozone-polluted cities in the country,' UPS District Manager Chris Martin said. 'This is one of the many ways UPS is operating our business in unison with our environmental objectives.'

Package flow technology leverages the tidal wave of digital information produced by scanning UPS 'smart labels' on nearly all of the 14 million packages moving through the company's global network each day. Consequently, delivery route planners know the night before what packages will need to be delivered to Sacramento residents and businesses the next day. By 'pushing' this data into a software program that plans driver routes, UPS can map out routes that require the fewest number of miles to complete.

The technology also helps decrease the number of missed deliveries, thereby reducing the need to drive back to an address a second time to deliver a package. This results in less fuel used and fewer CO_2 emissions. UPS is implementing package flow technology at more than 1000 package centres throughout the United States.

Deployment is scheduled to be completed in 2007.

Additionally, UPS's Sacramento fleet includes 112 of the company's compressed natural gas (CNG) alternative fuel delivery vehicles. UPS operates one of the largest alternative fuel fleets in North America with over 1700 such vehicles, including fuel cell, hybrid electric, electric, propane-powered, liquefied natural gas and CNG.

Source: Csrwire.com

Some initiatives, such as the UPS one described above, clearly have a direct impact on carbon footprint. Others, such as the use of virtual conferencing, may not. Do we use virtual conferencing as an *alternative* to travel, or as a *supplement*?

ACTIVITY

Find out what (if anything) your organization is doing to reduce its carbon footprint.

MANAGING THE COMMUNICATIONS BUDGET

Organizations use a number of methods to determine how much to spend on advertising (and other communications methods), including those outlined in this section.

Marginal analysis

This is an empirical research method, where a company runs a series of tests in different markets with different budgets to determine the best level of advertising expenditure. Each test is evaluated in terms of the marginal return generated by each pound or dollar of advertising budget.

Computers can then be used to generate quantitative mathematical models for budgeting and allocating advertising spend.

Arbitrary

If it feels good, do it! Despite the alternatives available, many organizations still allocate advertising spend on a 'gut feel' basis. This is, perhaps, not so strange, as it is difficult (if not impossible) to link the cost of advertising to any consequent increase in sales. There are simply too many variables affecting this (apparently straightforward) equation.

Affordable

If we have a budget, let us just spend it! Organizations might make some attempt to rank communications projects in terms of desirability or expected outcome, but the budget will be spent on all the projects it can afford.

Objective and task

The objective/task method (also known as the budget build-up method) is used by the majority of major national advertisers. The task method forces companies to think in terms of accomplishing goals.

The task method has three steps:

1. **Defining objectives** – The organization decides *exactly* what it wants the communications project to achieve and how that achievement will be measured.

2. **Determining strategy** – The communications strategy is developed, possibly based on the analysis of a number of alternatives, to achieve the objectives set.

3. **Estimating cost** – The strategy is costed out and the appropriate level of budget allocated. In this way the spend can (hopefully) be linked to the outcome.

The major drawback of this method is that it is usually very difficult to determine in advance how much money is needed to reach a specific goal. It is also almost impossible to tie any outcomes back to the strategy – too many variables (as always).

Percentage of sales

This is the simplest, and most popular, method because it is related to revenue levels and considered 'safe'. It may be based on a percentage of last year's sales, next year's anticipated sales or a combination of both.

The first problem is knowing what percentage of sales to use. Unfortunately, this is too often determined arbitrarily or is simply 'what we did last year'.

The second shortcoming is that it violates a basic marketing principle: marketing activities are supposed to 'stimulate' demand and thus sales; marketing activities are not supposed to occur as a 'result' of sales.

Competitive parity

Similar to the share of voice method (see below), but less sophisticated, the competitive parity approach is to 'match' communications pound-for-pound with a major competitor.

This method is flawed for a number of reasons:

- How can we determine what our competitors are spending? A company's annual accounts do not usually go into enough detail, and much of an organization's communications spend is incurred outside the marketing budget.

- Can we assume that our communications campaigns, even if they cost the same as those of a competitor, are as effective? We cannot even measure the effectiveness of our own communications, let alone those of our competitors!

Share of voice

A high correlation usually exists between a product or brand's share of a market and its share of industry advertising in markets with similar products. Many organizations believe it best to keep the 'share of voice' (measured in advertising minutes, or page coverage) ahead of market share.

This method is commonly used for new products, where a 'rule of thumb' such as 'the budget should be one and one half times the brand's expected share of market in 2 years' might be used. In other words, if the 2-year objective is a 10 per cent share of market, it should receive 15 per cent of the industry's advertising during the 2-year period.

The major hazard of this method is the tendency to become complacent. Companies must be aware of all their competitors' marketing activities, not just advertising. It also fails to look at the effectiveness of the marketing spend, so there is a temptation just to spend up to a budget, without spending wisely.

Centralized versus decentralized management

As with any organizational function, there is a continual stress between the benefits of centralization and decentralization in communications management. The main advantages of centralizing include the following:

- Centralization means control. It is much easier to make sure that communications activities meet their objectives, and those of the organization, if the management of the processes is centralized. Strong corporate policies and procedures can be implemented and results measured.

- Centralization means coordination. We have seen how important it is for consistency within the communications mix, and this is more likely to be achieved if the management process is centralized.

- Centralization means cost reduction. This is true not only because of tighter controls over expenditure but also because of economies of scale. There is a huge overlap between the components of the communications mix, and many of these can me eliminated (or at least reduced) by central management.

- Centralization means clear direction. Strategy is best set in one place, and one place only, otherwise people find the lack of goal congruence confusing and demotivating.

However, there are also strong arguments in favour of decentralized communications management:

- Decentralization means differentiation. Local markets have local needs, and decentralization avoids the risk of 'blanket' communications being directed at a diverse stakeholder audience with a wide range of differing needs and viewpoints.

- Decentralization means diversity. Having local empowerment within the marketing function allows a wide variety of staff to contribute their ideas and information.

- Decentralization means dynamism. Those closest to the stakeholder are best placed to react quickly to the changing environment. Whether it is a competitor campaign, or a change in stakeholder opinion, local management can change the elements of the communications mix to meet the challenge.

- Decentralization means drive. Staff are motivated by being given authority to act without reference to a centralized management structure. Motivated staff produce better results; they can be more creative, and are more productive.

Most organizations try to achieve a balance between the above approaches by implementing some form of 'think global, act local' structure. In this approach, policy and strategy are determined centrally, but individual communications activities are designed and implemented at the 'front end'. Such an approach necessarily sacrifices some of the benefits of each of the two extremes, in order to gain some of the benefits of the other. The optimal solution for each organization depends on its specific characteristics and constraints.

MEASURING THE SUCCESS OF COMMUNICATIONS ACTIVITIES

How can success be measured?

In considering which media to use within a communications campaign one of the factors that influences our choice is 'what has worked well in the past', so it is important that we can effectively evaluate what each medium has contributed towards the overall campaign results.

Accountants and marketers have long argued about the measurability and accountability of spending what is probably the single biggest expenditure that the organization makes.

Television is perhaps the most audited of the above-the-line tools (see the information about Nielsen, earlier in this unit). Day-by-day, minute-by-minute audience figures tell us who is watching at any time during the 24-hour day. Digital television has introduced two-way communication, so for the first time we can actually measure the audience's response by the number of 'red buttons' clicked. The inclusion of website addresses and direct response telephone numbers has also introduced a measurable aspect into television advertising.

But, in real terms, the role of advertising is to develop long-term brand values and the benefit of the expenditure can only be measured by a shift in customer attitudes over time. This is also true of all other above-the-line media in that although they all have a short-term measurable aspect to their use, their real value is as a strategic tool used consistently over time. It is not coincidence that some of the world's icon brands such as Coca-Cola, IBM and Kellogg's are also those that have consistently appeared in the top-ten advertising spend tables over the last 10 years.

Is it the role of marketing research to measure these shifts over time on both a brand/service level and within the marketplace? It is really the only way we get a complete picture of how customers perceive our offering.

There will always be significant debate about the validity and effectiveness of the advertising pound. We now have to communicate to compete and we are now in possession of more information than ever before. We now have to learn how that information can be used effectively.

Media exposure management

Within the promotional message, the evaluation has two elements to consider, the content of the message itself and how well that worked at communicating and the efficiency of the media chosen in transmitting the message.

The message content can be evaluated either by commissioning marketing research or by looking at the accuracy in the feedback we are getting from the consumer. If they are entering retail stores asking for the product or lots of people are walking round singing our jingle, we can assume the message is getting through.

The effectiveness of the media can also be measured by marketing research, but although we may be aware that awareness has risen to 80 per cent, how can we judge which media helped the most to achieve that?

Campaign measurement

Campaign measurement uses a basket of statistical metrics to try to determine the effect of a specific campaign on sales and profits. It uses data mining of complex databases to try to 'sift out' the effect of a campaign from the surrounding 'clutter' of environmental effects.

Increased sales

It is not appropriate to only look at sales when you are measuring the success of an advertisement or a campaign because other factors in the marketing mix or the external environment could affect sales (in either a negative or a positive way). For example, if there was media coverage of a research report suggesting that chocolate improved your IQ and reduced stress at the same time as the 'Chocco' advertising campaign, then this could be the reason for a sales increase and not the effect of the advertising campaign. Or, perhaps weather conditions could affect cocoa production adversely, which could cause price rises and reduce demand for 'Chocco', no matter how effective the advertising campaign.

Response rates

To measure the response to a sales promotion campaign that used a '20p off' coupon you could set up a system with retailers to count the number of redeemed vouchers. By media coding the coupon you will know which magazine produced the most responses.

Similarly, the response rates from direct marketing campaigns should be evaluated and, if appropriate, a further check made to calculate how much response is actually converted to sales. This way the cost of a campaign can be measured against the monetary gain from sales.

Conversion rates

One of the key measures of effectiveness is the conversion rate of 'prospect' to 'customer', in other words, what percentage of the audience actually move from awareness to action and make a purchase? As always, the problem is determining how many of the 'converts' made the decision to purchase as a result of the campaign and how many would have purchased anyway.

Order values

One of the effects of a successful communications campaign might be an increase in average order values. Communications campaigns are not just about persuading customers to buy but also to buy more.

Repeat orders

This is another version of the 'conversion rate' measure mentioned earlier. In this case, the conversion is from 'customer' to 'client' in the 'ladder of loyalty' (see Unit 2). Once again, the problem is determining just what caused the change in buyer behaviour.

ACTIVITIES

Practice work-based project

Communicating with stakeholders

Relationship marketing aims to form and sustain profitably mutually beneficial relationships by bringing together the organizational stakeholders and resources to deliver the best possible value proposition for the organization. In order to achieve this, it is important for the organization to develop a coordinated stakeholder communications plan. Two key stakeholders in any organization are suppliers and staff.

Role

You have been asked to present a proposal to the Corporate Communications Manager that contains a set of recommendations for improving stakeholder communications with specific reference to the organization's suppliers and staff.

Produce a formal report for your Corporate Communications Manager in which you

- Provide a brief background to your chosen organization, its products/ services, customer base, position in market, suppliers and staff (two sides of A4 maximum, to be included as an appendix).

- Analyse the power and interest of your organization's suppliers and staff and discuss situations in which each of these stakeholders might be classified as 'key players'.

- Identify the needs of suppliers, in terms of information from your organization and their relationship with it.

- Develop a coordinated communications plan that is responsive to the needs of your suppliers and adds value to the relationships.

- Develop a coordinated communications plan that might increase the level of 'employee engagement' within your organization.

- Identify and evaluate a range of methods that you could utilize to measure the success of your communications mix for each of the two stakeholder groups (suppliers and staff).

Notes on practice work-based project

Guidance on tackling the assignment

This assignment is an opportunity to use stakeholder analysis tools on the impact and influence of an internal and external stakeholder group on the development of relationship marketing at an operational level. Candidates are to recommend a communications mix for each stakeholder group.

Formal report

Relationship marketing concepts and theories should be appropriately applied to reflect understanding. The communications mixes should relate to operational marketing activity, and it is not expected that candidates suggest strategic options. Moreover, candidates should be creative in their suggestions and how they communicate these.

The report should include communication mixes to develop long-term relationships with the internal and external stakeholder groups identified in the question. This should include objectives, targets, tactics and proposed evaluation. Candidates should express their objectives as SMART objectives. Candidates should identify how to evaluate the success of their communications plans, and qualitative and quantitative methods should be considered. Candidates need to demonstrate the application of these measures in the context of the assignment. It is not sufficient to produce a generic series of measures, which may not be appropriate to the context.

In producing the report, it is important that the candidate adopts a structure and style that naturally lends themselves to reporting on the outcome of their study. The format and approach used will be driven by the relevant themes and emerging issues arising from the research. A formulaic task-based approach should be avoided. The examiners will be looking for a more holistic approach where there is clear evidence of insightful analysis, originality and clarity of expression. The report should be in a professional style with references to conceptual marketing theory included as appropriate.

Further work

- Taking two different countries, classify the 'national culture' of each (in respect of working practices) according to Hofstede's model. Discuss how you might use this knowledge to improve employee engagement in those countries?

- Investigate how your organization selects (evaluates/ranks for selection) and budgets for communications activities. How does it measure the effectiveness of those activities?

Hollingworth Leisure Centre

Hollingworth Leisure Centre is a not-for-profit leisure centre that has a fully equipped gymnasium, squash courts, fitness studio, swimming pool and provides beauty and holistic therapy treatments to the local community. Hollingworth Leisure Centre offers a range of fitness classes ranging from pilates to body pump. It has built up a good reputation for swimming teaching and moreover is the main local provider of swimming lessons for both adults and children in the area. The income from swimming lessons is approximately £400,000 per annum and this is re-invested in various projects such as updating the equipment and facilities. The gymnasium is run on a partnership basis with Fit Group who provide the equipment and are responsible for the maintenance and repair and Hollingworth Leisure Centre who provide the staff and marketing. The membership fees are split 50/50.

Hollingworth Leisure Centre is run by a small management team comprising a general manager and two assistant managers, who are responsible for the day-to-day operations and administration. The general manager reports to a Management Board of Trustees comprising local business people, and they report to a Trustee Board made up of local councillors, doctors, solicitors and members of the local community. Membership of the Management Board of Trustees and Trustee Board is voluntary. Hollingworth Leisure Centre employs 80 part-time staff ranging from fitness and swimming instructors to beauty therapists.

Hollingworth Leisure centre offers both peak and off peak (9.00 to 4.00pm) membership packages, and all new members pay a joining fee of £150.00. Members are entitled to use the full range of facilities. Hollingworth Leisure Centre only has a small marketing budget and places a weekly quarter page advertisement in the local paper and organizes several open days throughout the year. Research has indicated that personal word of mouth recommendation is extremely effective. A direct competitor Fitness First is due to open in 3 months time, and the general manager, Steven Hurst is considering conducting more marketing activities and implementing a loyalty scheme.

Questions

1. Identify the key stakeholders for Hollingworth Leisure Centre.

2. Develop a marketing communications plan to promote the swimming lessons to the local schools in the area.

3. Explain how Hollingworth Leisure Centre can use the member database to improve its service and develop customer relationships.

4. Recommend three types of sales promotions that could be used to recruit new members and explain how they will be evaluated.

Bibliography

Belbin, R.M. (1981) *Management teams: why they succeed or fail*, Butterworth Heinemann, Oxford.

Berry, L.L. (1995) Relationship marketing of services-Growing interest, emerging perspectives, *Journal of the Academy of Marketing Science*, **23**(4): 236–245.

Berry, L.L. and Parasuraman, A. (1992) *Marketing services: Competing through quality*, Free Press, Simon & Schuster.

Bliemel, F. and Eggert, A. (1998) Relationship marketing under fire, *Paper Presented at 6th International Colloquium in Relationship Marketing*, Auckland University, Auckland, 7–8 December.

Blyton, P. (1992) *The Handbook of HRM*, Blackwell Oxford: Business.

Elias, A.A. and Cavana, R.Y. (2000) Stakeholder analysis for systems thinking and modelling, available at http://www.mcs.vuw.ac.nz/opre/orsnz2000/papers/BobCavana.pdf.

Christopher, M. (2005) *Logistics and supply chain management – Creating value-adding networks*, 3rd Edition, Harlow, England: Prentice Hall-Financial Times.

Cox, A. (1996, March) Relational competence and strategic procurement management: Towards an entrepreneurial and contractual theory of the firm, *European Journal of Purchasing & Supply Management*, **2**(1): 57–70.

Cox, A. and Lamming, R. (1997, June) Managing supply in the firm of the future, *European Journal of Purchasing & Supply Management*, **3**(2): 53–62.

Dahlen, M., Lange, F. and Smith, T. (2010) *Marketing communications a brand narrative approach*, Chichester, England: John Wiley and Sons Ltd.

Deegan, D. (2001) *Managing activism, a guide to dealing with activists and pressure groups*, Kogan Page, London.

Evans, J.R. and Laskin, R.L. (1994, December) The relationship marketing process: A conceptualization and application, *Industrial Marketing Management*, **23**: 439–452.

Evans, P. and Wurster, T.S. (1999) *Blown to bits, how the new economics of information transforms strategy*, Boston, USA: Harvard Business School Press.

Fill, C. (2002) *Marketing communications, contexts, strategies and applications*, 3rd edition., Harlow, England: Prentice Hall-Financial Times.

Freeman, R.E. (1984) *Strategic management: A stakeholder approach*, Boston, USA: Pitman.

Gupta, S. (2006) Modeling customer lifetime value, *Journal of Service Research*, **9**(2): 139–155.

Gummesson, E. (1997) Relationship marketing as a paradigm shift: some conclusions from the 30R approach, *Management Decision*, **35**(4): 267–272.

Hackman, J.R., Oldham, G., Janson, R. and Purdy, K. (1975) *California Management Review*, **17**(4): 62.

Håkansson, H. (Eds.) (1987) *Industrial technological development: A network approach*, London: Croom Helm.

Handfield, R.B. and Nichols, E.L., Jr (2002) *Supply chain redesign: Transforming supply chains into integrated value system*, Upper Saddle River, NJ: Prentice-Hall.

Harland, C. (1996, March) Supply chain management: Relationships, chains and networks, *British Journal of Management*, **7**, Special Issue.

Heath, Robert L. (Ed.) (2001) *Handbook of public relations*, London: Sage.

Heskett, J.L., Jones, T.O., Loveman G.W., Sasser, W.E., Jr. & Schlesinger, L.A. (1994) Putting the service-profit chain to work, *Harvard Business Review*, **72** (March-April).

Hofstede, G. (1991) *Culture and organizations*, London: McGraw- Hill.

Kirkpatrick, D.L. (1998) *Evaluating training programs: The four levels*, USA: Berrett-Koehler.

Kotler, P. and Armstrong, C. (1994) *Principles of marketing*, 6th ed. Upper Saddle River, NJ: Prentice-Hall.

Kotler, P. and Lee, N. (2007) *Marketing in the public sector: A road map to improved performance*, Philadelphia: Wharton School Publishing.

Kotler, P. and Keller, K.L. (2006) *Marketing management*, Upper Saddle River, NJ: Pearson Education Inc.

MacGillivray, A. (2000) *The fair share*, London: New Economics Foundation.

McDonald, M. and Wilson, H. (2002) *The new marketing: Transforming the corporate future*, Butterworth-Heinemann.

Mendelow, A. (1991) *Stakeholder mapping, proceedings of the 2nd international conference on information systems*, Cambridge, MA.

Morgan, R. and Hunt, S. (1994) The commitment–trust theory of relationship marketing, *Journal of Marketing*, Vol. 58, Summer, pp. 20–28.

Oliver, R.W. (2000) The seven laws of e-commerce strategy, *Journal of Business Strategy*, September/October, pp. 8–10.

Overell, S. (2003) *On the scent of the right reward*, Financial Times, London.

Payne, A. (1995) *Advances in relationship marketing*, London: Kogan Page.

Pritchard. A (2003) *Education.com: An introduction to learning, teaching and ICT* (1-902466-00-4), London: ATL.

Quinn, J.B. and Hilmer, F.G. (1995) Strategic outsourcing: Make versus buy, *The McKinsey Quarterly*, 48–70.

Reicheld, F.F. and Sasser, W.E. (1990) Zero defects: Quality comes to services, *Harvard Business Review*, September–October, 105–13.

Ryan, D. and Jones, C. (2009) *Understanding digital marketing*, London, Kogan Page

Scholes, K. (1998) Stakeholder mapping: A practical tool for managers, in Johnson, G and Scholes, K. and Ambrosini, V (Eds.), *Exploring techniques of analysis and evaluation in strategic management*, London and New York: Pearson Higher Education.

Tapscott, D. and A. Williams (2006) *Wikinomics: How mass collaboration changes everything*, New York: Penguin.

Turngate, M. (2008) *Fashion brands: branding style from Armani to Zara*, London, Kogan Page

Index